WORLD OF ANIMALS

37

FISH

CATFISH

Sheatfish, Shark Catfish, Suckermouth Catfish ...

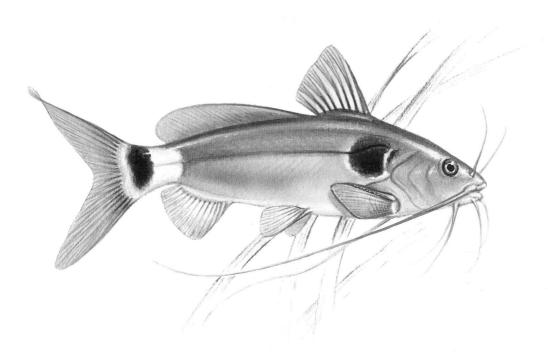

JOHN DAWES

an imprint of

SCHOLASTIC

www.scholastic.com/librarypublishing

Catfish are named for the catlike whiskers around the mouth. Shown here are a clown catfish (1) and an upside-down catfish (2).

Published 2005 by Grolier, an imprint of Scholastic Library Publishing Danbury, CT 06816

This edition published exclusively for the school and library market

The Brown Reference Group plc.
(incorporating Andromeda Oxford Limited)
8 Chapel Place
Rivington Street
London EC2A 3DQ

Project Directors: Graham Bateman, Lindsey Lowe
Editors: Marion Dent, Andrew Stilwell, John Woodward
Art Editor and Designer: Tony Truscott
Picture Managers: Helen Simm, Becky Cox
Picture Researcher: Alison Floyd
Main Artists: Denys Ovenden, Mick Loates, Colin Newman
Indexers: Michael and Marion Dent
Production: Alastair Gourlay, Maggie Copeland

Printed in Singapore

Set ISBN 0-7172-5905-6

Library of Congress Cataloging-in-Publication Data

Fish.
    p. cm. - - (World of Animals)
  Contents: vol. 31. Primitive fish -- vol. 32. Sharks -- vol. 33. Rays, chimaeras, and eels -- vol. 34. Carps, minnows, and allies -- vol. 35. Salmon, trout, and allies -- vol. 36. Cod, herring, and allies -- vol. 37. Catfish -- vol. 38. Piranhas -- vol. 39. Spiny-finned fish 1 -- vol. 40. Spiny-finned fish 2.
  ISBN 0-7172-5905-6 (set: alk. paper) -- ISBN 0-7172-5906-4 (vol. 31) -- ISBN 0-7172-5907-2 (vol. 32) --ISBN 0-7172-5908-0 (vol. 33) -- ISBN 0-7172-5909-9 (vol. 34) -- ISBN 0-7172-5910-2 (vol. 35) -- ISBN 0-7172-5911-0 (vol. 36) -- ISBN 0-7172-5912-9 (vol. 37) -- ISBN 0-7172-5913-7 (vol. 38) -- ISBN 0-7172-5914-5 (vol. 39) -- ISBN 0-7172-5915-3 (vol. 40)
  1. Fishes--Juvenile literature. I. Grolier (Firm) II. World of animals (Danbury, Conn.)

QL617.2.F55 2004
597--dc22

2004047333

About This Volume

Catfish get their name because the sensory whiskers around their mouths resemble a cat's whiskers. The whiskers, known as barbels, are perhaps the feature that most distinguishes catfish from other fish. Catfish are not the only fish to possess barbels, though; others, like the barbs, also have barbels. However, catfish have another special feature: the Weberian apparatus. This complex structure, consisting of modified bones that link the inner ear to the swim bladder, is a remarkable sound-receiver that gives catfish better hearing capabilities than most fish. Many catfish have another structure—an elastic spring mechanism—that can vibrate the swim bladder to create sounds. Some catfish also produce sounds by vibrating bones or rubbing them together. As a result, catfish are among the best "listeners" and "talkers" of the fish world. In some catfish the body is covered in hard bony plates of armor, often armed with spines, while in others the body is scaleless. These, and numerous other fascinating and sometimes spectacular arrangements, feature among the 2,500 or so species that make up the order Siluriformes, an especially interesting group of fish. This volume includes representative examples of most of the 34 families of catfish, from the smallest species, like the pygmy catfish at 1.4 inches (3.5 cm), to the wels, which may grow to 16.4 feet (5 m). It also describes sea-going catfish, venomous species, cave-dwelling types, and even blood-suckers.

2402

Contents

Armored catfish have rows of overlapping bony plates on the body.

The banjo catfish (1), driftwood catfish (2), and electric catfish (3) are mainly nocturnal feeders.

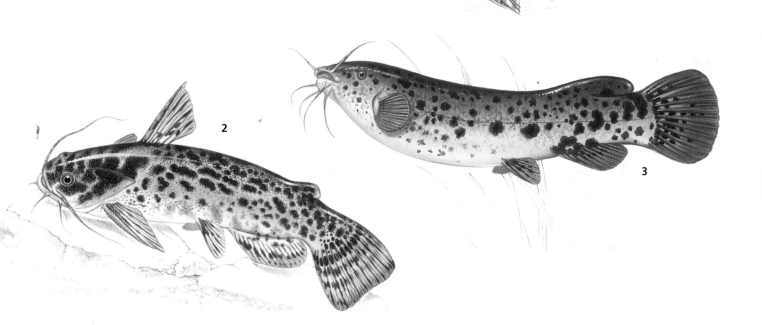

How to Use This Set

World of Animals: Fish is a 10-volume set that describes in detail fish from all around the world. Each volume features species that are grouped together because they share similar characteristics. So all the world's sharks are found in Volume 32, carplike fish are in Volume 34, catfish are in Volume 37, and so on. To help you find the volumes containing species that interest you, look at pages 6 and 7 (Find the Animal). A brief introduction to each volume is also given on page 2 (About This Volume).

Article Styles

Each volume contains two types of article. The first kind introduces major groups of fish (such as the ray-finned fish or the perchlike fish). This article reviews the variety of fish in the groups as well as their relationship with other groups of fish. The second type of article makes up most of each volume. It concentrates on describing in detail individual fish, such as the thornback ray, families of fish, such as hammerhead sharks, or groups of related families. Each such article starts with a fact-filled **data panel** to help you gather information at a glance. Used together, the two styles of article enable you to become familiar with specific fish in the context of their evolutionary history and biological relationships.

Data panel presents basic statistics of fish or fish group

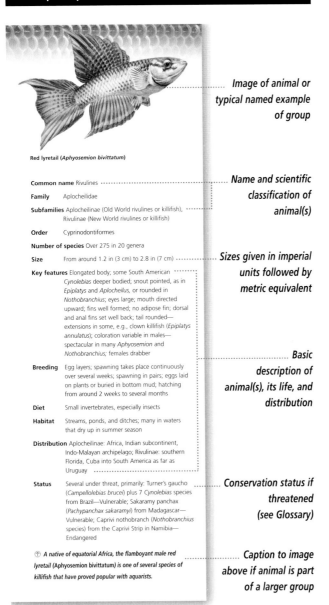

Red lyretail (*Aphyosemion bivittatum*)

Common name Rivulines ·········· → *Name and scientific classification of animal(s)*

Family Aplocheilidae

Subfamilies Aplocheilinae (Old World rivulines or killifish), Rivulinae (New World rivulines or killifish)

Order Cyprinodontiformes

Number of species Over 275 in 20 genera

Size From around 1.2 in (3 cm) to 2.8 in (7 cm) ·········· → *Sizes given in imperial units followed by metric equivalent*

Key features Elongated body; some South American *Cynolebias* deeper bodied; snout pointed, as in *Epiplatys* and *Aplocheilus*, or rounded in *Nothobranchius*; eyes large; mouth directed upward; fins well formed; no adipose fin; dorsal and anal fins set well back; tail rounded—extensions in some, e.g., clown killifish (*Epiplatys annulatus*); coloration variable in males—spectacular in many *Aphyosemion* and *Nothobranchius*; females drabber

Breeding Egg layers; spawning takes place continuously over several weeks; spawning in pairs; eggs laid on plants or buried in bottom mud; hatching from around 2 weeks to several months ·········· → *Basic description of animal(s), its life, and distribution*

Diet Small invertebrates, especially insects

Habitat Streams, ponds, and ditches; many in waters that dry up in summer season

Distribution Aplocheilinae: Africa, Indian subcontinent, Indo-Malayan archipelago; Rivulinae: southern Florida, Cuba into South America as far as Uruguay

Status Several under threat, primarily: Turner's gaucho (*Campellolebias brucei*) plus 7 *Cynolebias* species from Brazil—Vulnerable; Sakaramy panchax (*Pachypanchax sakaramyi*) from Madagascar—Vulnerable; Caprivi nothobranch (*Nothobranchius* species) from the Caprivi Strip in Namibia—Endangered ·········· → *Conservation status if threatened (see Glossary)*

ⓐ *A native of equatorial Africa, the flamboyant male red lyretail (Aphyosemion bivittatum) is one of several species of killifish that have proved popular with aquarists.* ·········· → *Caption to image above if animal is part of a larger group*

→ *Image of animal or typical named example of group*

Article describes a particular fish or group of fish

Scientific name of animal

Common name of animal

Captions to photographs provide additional information about each animal's lifestyle

SHARKS

Gray Reef Shark

Carcharhinus amblyrhynchos

Like many other animals, the gray reef shark sends out unmistakable visual messages when it feels threatened. If these signals are ignored, the shark may attack with devastating consequences.

Common name Gray reef shark (long-nosed blacktail shark)

Scientific name Carcharhinus amblyrhynchos

Family Carcharhinidae

Order Carcharhiniformes

Size Up to 8.4 ft (2.6 m) but usually smaller

Key features Sleek, dark-gray or bronze-gray back fading to white on the underside; long snout with underslung mouth; caudal fin has distinct black edge (hence one of the shark's common names); some individuals have white-tipped first dorsal fin (they are regarded as *C. wheeleri* by some authorities)

Breeding Internal fertilization; embryos develop a placenta through which they obtain nourishment for up to 1 year; 1–6 pups produced in a litter

Diet Wide range of bony fish, as well as squid, octopuses, lobsters, and crabs

Habitat On continental and island shelves and on coral reefs, preferring deeper waters around the dropoff zone (where the reef plunges sharply at its ocean-facing edge); also found in atoll passes and in shallower areas with strong currents

Distribution Widely distributed in tropical zones of both the Pacific and Indian Oceans; if *C. wheeleri* is accepted as being a separate from *C. amblyrhynchos*, then the range extends into the Red Sea and down as far as South Africa

World population Abundant at many locations within its range, but may be declining in some areas

WHEN THREATENED, MANY ANIMALS EXPERIENCE a rush of adrenalin that prepares them to attack or flee. In such a situation sharks like the gray reef shark send out an unmistakable warning message to those around them. We ignore such powerful "fight or flight" signals at our peril.

Threat and Attack

The gray reef shark is not among the largest of sharks, neither is it indiscriminately aggressive. It is, nonetheless, one of the species most frequently implicated in attacks on humans. That is not because the shark actively seeks out an unsuspecting victim to attack. It is because the species appears to define a territory around itself—a "personal space"—and reacts quite forcefully if it feels it is being threatened.

For this reason divers that encounter this wide-ranging shark are advised not to approach it rapidly, not to get too close, and not to startle it by sudden movements or noises. In any of these situations many other sharks would take flight. However, the gray reef shark will often not just stand its ground but will go into a characteristic series of body movements that leaves the observer or intruder in no doubt that the shark feels threatened.

If the intruder persists, it is likely that the display will intensify, culminating sooner or later in an attack. However, if the messages being sent out by the shark are read and understood, and a careful retreat is made, the risk of attack subsides. The shark may also retreat once it no longer feels threatened.

It appears that such encounters occur with greater frequency when a lone gray reef shark

ⓐ As [...] approa[...] gray [...] out [...] nee[...] N[...]

48 · **SEE ALSO** Sharks, Ground **32**:42

Cross-references to relevant pages in this and other volumes ··········

Easy-to-read and comprehensive text

A number of other features help you navigate through the volumes and present you with helpful extra information. At the bottom of many pages are **cross-references** to other articles of interest. They may be to related fish, fish that live in similar places, fish with similar behavior, predators (or prey), and much more. Each volume also contains a **Set Index** to the complete *World of Animals: Fish*. Most fish mentioned in the text are indexed by common and scientific names, and many topics are also covered. There is also a **Glossary** that will help you if there are words in the text that you do not fully understand. Each volume includes a list of useful **Further Reading and Websites** that help you take your research further. On page 7 you will find a complete checklist of all the fish superclasses, classes, and orders of the world and where they are featured in the set.

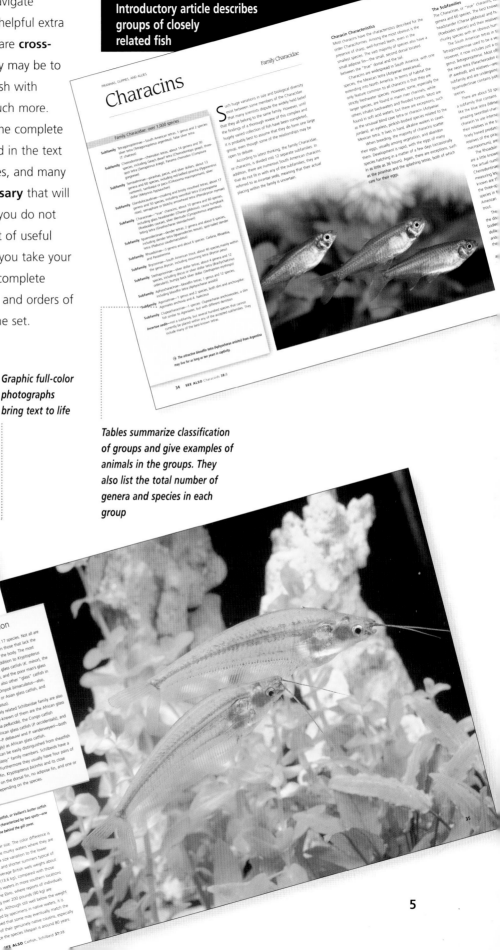

Graphic full-color photographs bring text to life

Tables summarize classification of groups and give examples of animals in the groups. They also list the total number of genera and species in each group

At-a-glance boxes cover topics of special interest

Find the Animal

World of Animals: Fish is the fourth part of a library that describes all groups of living animals. Each cluster of volumes in World of Animals covers a familiar group of animals—mammals, birds, reptiles, amphibians, fish, and insects and other invertebrates. These groups also represent categories of animals recognized by scientists (see The Animal Kingdom below).

Rank	Scientific name	Common name
Phylum	Chordata	Animals with a backbone
Superclass	Gnathostomata	Jawed fish
Class	Actinopterygii	Ray-finned fish
Order	Characiformes	Characoids
Family	Characidae	Characins
Genus	*Pygocentrus*	Piranhas
Species	*natereri*	Red-bellied piranha

The Animal Kingdom

The living world is divided into five kingdoms, one of which (kingdom Animalia) is the main subject of the World of Animals. Kingdom Animalia is divided into numerous major groups called phyla, but only one of them (Chordata) contains animals that have a backbone. Chordates, or vertebrates, include animals like mammals, birds, reptiles, amphibians, and fish. There are about 38,000 species of vertebrates, while the phyla that contain animals without backbones (so-called invertebrates, like insects and spiders) include at least 1 million species. To find which set of volumes in the World of Animals you need to choose, see the chart below.

Fish in Particular

World of Animals: Fish provides a broad survey of some of the most abundant, unusual, varied, and yet rarely seen creatures on our planet. Fish are unique among vertebrates because all species live in water—although some have adapted to spend periods on land. Fish are

The kingdom Animalia is subdivided into groups such as classes, families, genera, and species. Above is the classification of the red-bellied piranha.

divided into major groups called superclasses, classes, and orders. The two superclasses comprise the jawless and the jawed fish. Different classes include fish such as lobe-finned fish, cartilaginous fish, and ray-finned fish. In each class there are often a number of fish orders, and in the orders there are families. All the fish superclasses, classes, and orders are shown on page 7; the common names of some of the most important species in these groups are also listed.

Fish classification is a changing science. Not only have several different ways of grouping fish already been proposed, but new evidence, such as from DNA analysis, has resulted in a major rethinking of the fish family tree;

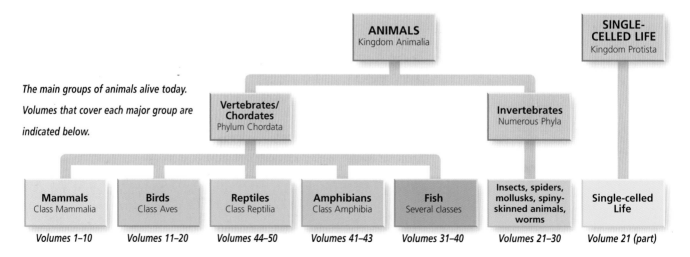

The main groups of animals alive today. Volumes that cover each major group are indicated below.

ANIMALS
Kingdom Animalia

SINGLE-CELLED LIFE
Kingdom Protista

Vertebrates/ Chordates
Phylum Chordata

Invertebrates
Numerous Phyla

Mammals Class Mammalia	**Birds** Class Aves	**Reptiles** Class Reptilia	**Amphibians** Class Amphibia	**Fish** Several classes	Insects, spiders, mollusks, spiny-skinned animals, worms	**Single-celled Life**
Volumes 1–10	*Volumes 11–20*	*Volumes 44–50*	*Volumes 41–43*	*Volumes 31–40*	*Volumes 21–30*	*Volume 21 (part)*

the result is that some species are now placed in different groups by different scientists. Furthermore, the same fish may have a different name under different systems of classification. Therefore the system of classification in this set may differ from others and may itself change as the results of new studies emerge. The system followed mostly here is the one devised by Joseph S. Nelson in *Fishes of the World* (John Wiley & Sons, Inc., 1994).

Naming Fish

To discuss animals, names are needed for the different kinds. Red-bellied piranhas are one kind of fish and black-spot piranhas another. All red-bellied piranhas look alike, breed together, and produce young like themselves. This distinction corresponds closely to the zoologists' definition of a species. All red-bellied piranhas belong to one species, and all black-spot piranhas belong to another species.

Most animals have different names in different languages. Therefore zoologists use an internationally recognized system for naming species consisting of two-word scientific names, usually in Latin or Greek. The red-bellied piranha is called *Pygocentrus natereri* and the black-spot piranha *Pygocentrus cariba*. *Pygocentrus* is the name of the genus (a group of very similar species) that includes red-bellied and black-spot piranhas; *natereri* or *cariba* indicates the species in the genus. The same scientific names are recognized the world over. This allows for precision and helps avoid confusion. However, a species may have more than one scientific name—it may have been described and named at different times without the zoologists realizing it was one species.

FISH SUPERCLASSES, CLASSES, AND ORDERS

SUPERCLASS AGNATHA	**jawless fish**
Order Petromyzontiformes **(Vol. 31)**	lampreys
Order Myxiniformes **(Vol. 31)**	hagfish
SUPERCLASS GNATHOSTOMATA	**jawed fish**
CLASS CHONDRICHTHYES	**cartilaginous fish**
Order Heterodontiformes **(Vol. 32)**	bullhead sharks
Order Orectolobiformes **(Vol. 32)**	carpet sharks
Order Carcharhiniformes **(Vol. 32)**	ground sharks
Order Lamniformes **(Vol. 32)**	mackerel sharks
Order Hexanchiformes **(Vol. 32)**	frilled and cow sharks
Order Squaliformes **(Vol. 32)**	dogfish sharks
Order Squatiniformes **(Vol. 32)**	angel sharks
Order Pristiophoriformes **(Vol. 32)**	saw sharks
Order Rajiformes **(Vol. 33)**	rays
Order Chimaeriformes **(Vol. 33)**	chimaeras
CLASS SARCOPTERYGII	**lobe-finned fish**
Order Coelacanthiformes **(Vol. 31)**	coelacanths
Order Ceratodontiformes **(Vol. 31)**	Australian lungfish
Order Lepidosirenifomes **(Vol. 31)**	South American and African lungfish
CLASS ACTINOPTERYGII	**ray-finned fish**
Order Polypteriformes **(Vol. 31)**	bichirs and ropefish
Order Acipenseriformes **(Vol. 31)**	sturgeons and paddlefish
Order Amiiformes **(Vol. 31)**	bowfin
Order Semionotiformes **(Vol. 31)**	garfish
Order Osteoglossiformes **(Vol. 31)**	bonytongues and allies
Order Elopiformes **(Vol. 31)**	tarpons
Order Albuliformes **(Vol. 33)**	spiny eels
Order Anguilliformes **(Vol. 33)**	eels
Order Saccopharyngiformes **(Vol. 33)**	swallow and gulper eels
Order Clupeiformes **(Vol. 36)**	herring and allies
Order Cypriniformes **(Vol. 34)**	carp and minnows
Order Characiformes **(Vol. 38)**	characins and allies
Order Siluriformes **(Vol. 37)**	catfish
Order Gymnotiformes **(Vol. 33)**	New World knifefish
Order Esociformes **(Vol. 35)**	pikes, pickerels, and mudminnows
Order Osmeriformes **(Vol. 35)**	smelts and allies
Order Salmoniformes **(Vol. 35)**	salmon, trout, and allies
Order Stomiiformes **(Vol. 35)**	dragonfish and allies
Order Ateleopodiformes **(Vol. 35)**	jellynose fish
Order Aulopiformes **(Vol. 35)**	lizardfish
Order Myctophiformes **(Vol. 35)**	lanternfish
Order Lampridiformes **(Vol. 35)**	oarfish
Order Polymixiiformes **(Vol. 35)**	beardfish
Order Percopsiformes **(Vol. 36)**	trout-perches and allies
Order Ophidiiformes **(Vol. 36)**	cusk eels and brotulas
Order Gadiformes **(Vol. 36)**	cod and allies
Order Batrachoidiformes **(Vol. 36)**	toadfish
Order Lophiiformes **(Vol. 36)**	anglerfish and allies
Order Mugiliformes **(Vol. 38)**	mullets
Order Atheriniformes **(Vol. 38)**	rainbowfish and silversides
Order Beloniformes **(Vol. 38)**	flying fish and ricefish
Order Cyprinodontiformes **(Vol. 38)**	piranhas, guppies, and allies
Order Stephanoberyciformes **(Vol. 39)**	pricklefish and allies
Order Beryciformes **(Vol. 39)**	fangtooths and allies
Order Zeiformes **(Vol. 39)**	dories and allies
Order Gasterosteiformes **(Vol. 39)**	sticklebacks, sea horses, and allies
Order Synbranchiformes **(Vol. 33)**	swamp eels and allies
Order Mastacembeliformes **(Vol. 33)**	spiny eels
Order Scorpaeniformes **(Vol. 39)**	mail-cheeked fish
Order Perciformes **(Vol. 40)**	perchlike fish
Order Pleuronectiformes **(Vol. 39)**	flatfish
Order Tetraodontiformes **(Vol. 39)**	triggers, puffers, and allies

WHAT IS A CATFISH?

Catfish are one of the easiest groups of fish to identify due to the sensory barbels, or "whiskers," that give rise to the "cat" part of their common name. Most catfish have four pairs of barbels, and the usual arrangement is for one pair to be located on the head, one on the upper jaw, and two on the chin. However, there are many variations. Some species, like the giant catfish (*Pangasius gigas*), have reduced barbels, while others may lack one or more pairs—but never all four. In other types, such as the long-whiskered catfish (family Pimelodidae), some of the barbels may be longer than the body. In yet others, like the squeakers or upside-down catfish (family Mochokidae), the barbels may be elaborate and even "feathery."

Although barbels are a distinctive feature of catfish, other species of fish also have them. Carp (*Cyprinus carpio*), barbs (*Barbus* species), and even some sharks are all examples of noncatfish species that have barbels. Another fish, the barbel (*Barbus barbus*), even gets its common name from the distinctive feature. For this reason it is a combination of features, rather than simply the possession of barbels, that identifies a species as a catfish. Most of the features, though, are skeletal and cannot be directly observed in living specimens.

⊖ *The decorated sino (Synodontis decorus) from the Upper Zaire and Cameroon regions in Africa may grow up to 12 inches (30 cm) in length. Like some other squeaker catfish, it sometimes swims upside down.*

There are 34 living families of catfish, plus one fossil one. Together they form the order Siluriformes. Over 410 genera and about 2,500 species have been identified. Here we feature 21 of the 34 families.

Remarkable Sound Machine

One of the most important features of catfish is the complex bony structure, the Weberian apparatus, linking the swim bladder to the inner ear. The apparatus consists of small bones (ossicles) that transmit changes in the volume of the bladder to the inner ear. When the volume of the swim bladder changes—as it does when it receives sound vibrations—that affects the internal pressure in the bladder, which, in turn, sends information to the inner ear.

The Weberian apparatus enhances the sound waves catfish pick up from their environment. This is particularly important for species that live in turbid water. By combining the benefits rendered by the Weberian apparatus with the sensory

information picked up via the barbels, many catfish can not only survive but actually thrive in low-visibility, silt-laden conditions that numerous other fish would find intolerable.

In some catfish the swim bladder has an additional function: sound production. A structure known as the elastic spring mechanism can make the swim bladder vibrate and produce sounds. Some types of catfish use this, or other sound-producing mechanisms, to such an extent that they form one of the most distinctive characteristics of the species. Consequently, they are referred to as talking, squeaking, or croaking catfish.

Catfish Self-protection

Another characteristic of many catfish is a two-spine locking mechanism on the dorsal (back) fin. The first spine is sometimes so small that it is barely visible to the naked eye, but the second is always prominent. When a catfish is disturbed, one of its instinctive reactions is to spread out its fins. As it does so, the first dorsal spine locks the second one in an upright position. Simultaneously, spines are raised on other fins. The actions, together with the tough scales (scutes) or body armor that many species also possess, make many catfish difficult prey items.

In a number of species fin spines are not just physical defensive structures but contain venomous chemicals. In such species it is the pectoral (chest) fin spines that are particularly important, rather than the dorsal ones. Most catfish species that can inflict injury with their spines (some of which are saw-edged) are called "passive stingers." In other words, they do not actively search out a victim but raise their spines if they are threatened, bitten by a predator, picked up, or stepped on. In some species generally regarded as passive stingers, like the madtoms (*Noturus* species), toxicity produced by venomous glands adds to the dangers of being stung.

Other species, including the Asian stinging catfish (*Heteropneustes fossilis*), are more aggressive and will actively seek out victims. The sting of such "active stingers" is not just extremely painful but may also have more serious consequences. Even more potent is the venom possessed by the marine catfish of the genus *Plotosus*, whose sting can actually result in death. Most venomous species of catfish, though, like the long-whiskered catfish or pims (family Pimelodidae), are only mildly poisonous.

⬇ *The excellent protection provided by the body armor of scarlet catfish (Pseudoacanthicus species) can be seen in the example below.*

Other Features

Most catfish have a second dorsal fin known as the adipose fin. In some species the adipose fin may be quite large, even sail-like, for example, in the bagrids (family Bagridae) and the squeakers or upside-down catfish (family Mochokidae).

In members of the family Siluridae, the spiny dwarf catfish (family Scoloplacidae), the whale catfish (family Cetopsidae), the banjo catfish (family Aspredinidae), and the little-known, single-species family Nematogenyidae, the adipose fin is absent. In the suckermouth armored catfish (family Loricariidae) and the parasitic catfish (family Trichomycteridae) the adipose fin may or may not be present. In the airsac catfish (family Heteropneustidae) the adipose fin is either absent or is present as a low ridge. In some of the the torrent catfish (family Amblycipitidae) the adipose fin joins up with the caudal (tail) fin, and in the air-breathing catfish (family Clariidae) the dorsal and caudal fin may also be joined.

Size Differences

Catfish also vary widely in terms of size. At one extreme there are giants like the wels (*Silurus glanis*)—which frequently attains a length of 10 feet (3 m) but has reportedly been recorded at 16.4 feet (5 m)—and the giant catfish, which can grow to 6.5 feet (2 m). At the other end of the size scale there are tiny species such as the pygmy catfish (*Corydoras pygmaeus*), which is fully mature at a mere 1.4 inches (3.5 cm).

Varied Egg Laying

All catfish are oviparous (lay eggs). In most cases both eggs and sperm are released into the water, where external fertilization takes place. However, in a few instances, notably among the driftwood catfish (family Auchenipteridae), fertilization actually takes place within the body of the female, after which the eggs are laid. Although catfish fertilization is usually external, various species have developed methods to increase the chances of it happening successfully and also to ensure the eggs survive to the point of hatching or beyond. For example, in the members of the genus *Corydoras* females actually drink sperm, pass it rapidly down the gut, and eject it onto a small clutch of eggs that they nestle between their pelvic fins. In others the usual strategy is to release sperm and eggs simultaneously, or in sequence, in a specially prepared nest, or to scatter them among vegetation.

Despite the wide diversity of strategies employed by catfish, they can all be grouped under three main types. The first type has neither a nest nor parental care of eggs or young. The second involves construction of a nest and some degree of parental care of eggs, but not of young. The last type involves nest construction and care of both eggs and young.

Who's Who Among the Catfish?

Order Siluriformes

Family Diplomystidae—2 genera, 3 species; the only living catfish with teeth in the upper jaw; also known as diplomystid catfish

Family Hypsidoridae—1 species; fossil family with teeth in the upper jaw

Family Ictaluridae—7 genera, about 45 species; includes the well-known channel catfish (*Ictalurus punctatus*); also known as ictalurids or North American freshwater catfish*

Family Bagridae—30 genera, about 210 species; includes the large giraffe catfish (*Auchenoglanis occidentalis*); also known as bagrid catfish*

Family Olyridae—1genus, 4 species; members of the family have a pointed tail, which is unusual in catfish; also known as bannertail catfish

Family Cranoglanididae—1 genus, probably 1 species; has bony plates on top of the head; also known as armorhead catfish

Family Siluridae—about 12 genera, about 100 species; includes the wels (*Silurus glanis*) as well as the unusual glass catfish (*Kryptopterus bicirrhis*); also known as sheatfish or sheat catfish*

Family Schilbeidae—about 18 genera, 45–60 species; includes the striped schilbe catfish (*Schilbe mystus*); also known as schilbeid or schilbid catfish*

Family Pangasiidae—probably 2 genera, 25 species; contains the iridescent shark (*Pangasius hypophthalmus*), popular with aquarium keepers, and the giant or Mekong catfish (*Pangasius gigas*); also known as shark catfish*

Family Amphiliidae—7 genera, around 47 species; divided into 2 subfamilies; also known as African hillstream or loach catfish

Family Sisoridae (Bagariidae)—about 20 genera, 100 species; also known as Asian hillsteam or sisorid catfish*

Family Amblycipitidae—2 genera, about 10 species; some species have joined adipose and caudal fins; also known as torrent catfish

Family Akysidae—3 genera, about 13 species; 1 genus (*Breitensteinia*) lacks an adipose fin; also known as stream catfish

Family Parakysidae—1 genus, 2 species; sometimes grouped with the family Akysidae; lower jaw barbels may be divided

Family Chacidae—1 genus, 3 species; have flat, broad head and compressed body; also known as squarehead, angler, or frogmouth catfish*

Family Clariidae—about 13 genera, 100 species; have a specially modified breathing organ that gives the family its common name; also known as air-breathing or walking catfish*

Family Heteropneustidae (Saccobranchidae)—1 genus, probably only 1 species, the highly venomous *Heteropneustes fossilis;* also known as stinging, liver, fossil, or airsac catfish*

Family Malapteruridae—1 genus, 11 species; includes the potentially dangerous *Malapterurus electricus;* also known as electric catfish*

Family Ariidae—about 14 genera, 120–150 species; despite common name, some members represented in freshwater and brackish habitats, e.g., the shark catfish (*Arius jordani* and *A. seemani*); also known as sea catfish*

Family Plotosidae—about 9 genera, 32 species; some members have venomous spines; also known as eeltail or tandan catfish*

Family Mochokidae—10 genera, about 170 species; includes the interesting members of the genus *Synodontis* from Africa; also known as squeaking or upside-down catfish*

Family Doradidae—about 35 genera, 80–100 species; includes the sound-producing talking catfish (*Amblydoras hancocki*); also known as doradids or thorny catfish*

Family Ageneiosidae:—2 genera, about 12 species; all have short barbels despite one of the common names—barbelless catfish; also known as bottlenose catfish

Family Auchenipteridae—about 21 genera, 65–75 species; some species in the family build bubble nests; egg fertilization may be internal; also known as driftwood catfish*

Family Pimelodidae—about 56 genera, 300 species; some species have exceptionally long barbels; also known as long-whiskered catfish or pims*

Family Cetopsidae: 4–7 genera, about 12–23 species depending on classification system; also known as whale catfish*

Family Helogeneidae—1–3 genera, 4 species; included within the family Cetopsidae by some authorities; members of family have a bullet-shaped head; also known as marbled catfish*

Family Hypophthalmidae—1 genus, 2 or 3 species; also known as lookdown or loweye catfish

Family Aspredinidae—about 12 genera, 29 species; includes "jet-propelled" species and is divided into several subfamilies; also known as banjo catfish

Family Nematogenyidae:—1 genus, 1 species; considered a subfamily of the parasitic catfish (family Trichomycteridae) by some authorities; also known as parasitic catfish

Family Trichomycteridae—about 36 genera,155 species; divided into as many as 8 subfamilies; not all species are parasitic; also known as parasitic or pencil catfish*

Family Callichthyidae—8 genera, over 208 species; divided into 2 subfamilies. It includes many species popular among aquarists; also known as armored catfish*

Family Scoloplacidae—1genus, 4 species; body has 2 rows of spine-bearing plates; also known as spring dwarf catfish

Family Loricariidae—about 80 genera, 550–600 species; large family divided into 5 subfamilies; also known as suckermouth armored catfish*

Family Astroblepidae—2 genera, about 40 species; sometimes classified as family Argidae or placed within the family Loricariidae; also known as climbing catfish

⊖ *Striped catfish (Plotosus lineatus) of the Indo-Pacific region carry venom in their fin spines that can cause death to humans unfortunate enough to be stung by them.*

* Denotes coverage in the volume

Channel catfish (*Ictalurus punctatus*)

Common name North American freshwater catfish

Family Ictaluridae

Order Siluriformes

Number of species Around 45 in 7 genera

Size From 4 in (10 cm) long madtoms to 19–65 in (48–165 cm) long channel catfish

Key features Body moderately elongated and scaleless; 4 pairs of barbels; teeth "velvety" pads (except toothless blindcat—no teeth); stout spine at front of dorsal fin (except in *Prietella*); tail straight or round to moderately forked; adipose fin small and well separated from caudal in most species; in madtoms and stonecat it is long, low, and either joined or almost joined to caudal; madtoms and stonecat can produce venom; all species except widemouth blindcat and toothless blindcat have swim bladders; blindcats have no eyes

Breeding Nests saucer-shaped depressions or scrapings under overhangs, among vegetation, or in cavities; built by one or both spawners and vigorously defended; eggs: as few as 15 in madtoms and up to 10,000 in larger species; guarded by male, but female may play a role; hatching from 5–14 days depending on species and water temperature

Diet Aquatic invertebrates and other small fish; carrion may be taken

Habitat Rivers and lakes with sandy or muddy bottoms; some madtoms prefer fast-flowing waters; blind species prefer artesian wells

Distribution North and Central America from Hudson Bay and St. Lawrence drainages in Canada southward to the Rio Ucumacinta in Guatemala

Status Several species face varying threats to survival

⊕ *The channel catfish (Ictalurus punctatus) lives in rivers, large creeks, ponds, and reservoirs mainly in southern Canada and the east-central U.S., although it has been introduced elsewhere. It is a popular sport and food fish.*

CATFISH

North American Freshwater Catfish

Ictaluridae

The white catfish found in North America was the first fish to be identified and named as a catfish.

IN 1816 THE FRENCH NATURALIST Baron Georges Cuvier (1769–1832), inspired by the fish's barbels or "whiskers," described the white catfish (*Ameiurus catus*) as a *poisson-chat* or "fish-cat," which translates into English as catfish. The label stuck, and today all the 2,500 or so species that form the order Siluriformes are known as catfish.

The family to which the white catfish belongs is the Ictaluridae. All ictalurids share a number of important features. The most notable is the total absence of scales and the possession of four pairs of well-formed sensory barbels. One pair, the maxillary barbels, arises from the upper jaw. Two pairs come from the lower jaw or chin and are called the mandibular or mental barbels. Another pair forms in the region of the "nose," so are known as the nasal barbels. Together the barbels give ictalurids their distinctly whiskery appearance.

Family Groups

The family Ictaluridae is organized into five groups. First is the channel catfish (genus *Ictalurus*), consisting of about nine species. Second come the bullheads

(genus *Ameiurus*), of which there are seven species. The third group covers approximately 25 species of madtom and stonecat (genus *Noturus*). There is only a single species, the toothless blindcat (*Trogloglanis pattersoni*), in the fourth group. The fifth group, the flathead catfish, is made up of three genera: *Prietella*, which consists of two species, and *Pylodictis* and *Satan*, which have a single species each.

The five groups make up a family that is commonly known as the North American freshwater catfish or the bullhead catfish. While the first of the names does not roll off the tongue quite so easily as the second, it is the more accurate of the two. Bullhead is best reserved for the genus *Ameiurus*, most of whose species are known as bullheads.

⊕ The four pairs of barbels characteristic of all North American freshwater catfish can clearly be seen around the head and mouth of these brown bullhead catfish (Ictalurus nebulosus). The similarity of the barbels to a cat's whiskers inspired the name catfish.

Similar but Different

The first two groups, the channel catfish and the bullheads, are superficially quite similar to each other. In fact, the similarities were once considered to be so close that the bullheads were believed to be a subgenus of the channel catfish. Perhaps the most easily distinguished characteristics between the two relate to the eyes and the caudal and anal fins.

The channel catfish have fairly large eyes; but in bullheads the eyes are smaller. The caudal fin is moderately or deeply forked in channel catfish but rounded, straight, or slightly notched in bullheads—with the exception of the white catfish, which has a moderately forked tail. The anal fin in channel catfish generally has more rays—33 to 35 compared with the bullheads' 17 to 27—but as with the caudal fin, there is a little overlap.

The third group, the madtoms, are all smaller than their cousins, with one notable exception, the stonecat (*Noturus flavus*), which can grow to a little over 12 inches (30 cm). All the others are around the 4-inch (10-cm) mark. In the madtoms the adipose fin is long and low, and is either joined to or only slightly separated from the caudal fin, which is slightly rounded or straight. By comparison, in the channel catfish and the bullheads the adipose fin is small and well separated from the caudal fin.

There are three blind members in the family. One, the toothless blindcat, has a rounded head. The other two blind species, the widemouth blindcat (*Satan eurystomus*) and the Mexican blindcat (*Prietella phreatophila*), both have flat heads. They are closely related to each other and are included, along with the flathead catfish (*Pylodictis olivaris*), in the group called flathead catfish.

Territorial Breeders

Although breeding data for some species is lacking, especially in the case of the blind forms, the family has several features in

⊕ *A brown bullhead catfish (Ameiurus nebulosus). The bullheads and channel catfish are very alike, but one distinguishing feature that separates them is the nature of the caudal fin.*

common. Territories can be established at various times of year outside the breeding season. The most dominant individuals hold the largest and best territories, which they defend by displays and probably by scent. Individuals can apparently identify each other and so maintain their place in the hierarchical order.

With the start of the breeding season territorial activity becomes more intense, but not necessarily centered around previously held territories. Instead, in the channel catfish and bullheads the fish migrate to shallower water. Madtoms may move into pools or close to the head of shallow, fast-flowing stretches of water.

Nests are excavated, usually by the males and often in vegetated areas, under overhangs or under logs. Madtoms may lay as few as 15 or as many as 300 eggs, with females splitting their egg laying and depositing half in one male's nest and half in another's. Stonecats may produce 1,000 eggs, and in larger species in the family as many as 10,000 may be laid.

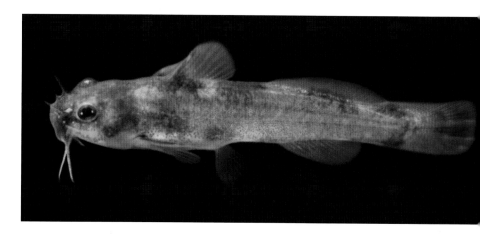

Responsibility for guarding the eggs can be either the male's alone or can be shared with the female. Where both sexes take on the responsibility, the male may patrol the periphery of the territory (as happens with bullheads), while the female mouths and fans the eggs. In madtoms it is usually the male that looks after the eggs, rolling them over and mouthing them to keep them clean and well aerated.

⊕ *The Ozark madtom (Noturus albater). Madtoms may be small, but they produce venom similar to a bee sting to ward off predators.*

Clever Channel Cats

If we were to draw up an animal intelligence ranking, most of us would place mammals and birds well above fish. However, some species, such as the channel catfish (*Ictalurus punctatus*), can learn to perform tasks or avoid "punishment" in the same way that a laboratory mouse can.

The channel catfish performs well in the intelligence stakes. An experiment was set up in which a variety of fish species were faced with the challenge of having to move from one part of an aquarium to another when a light was switched on to avoid receiving a mild electric shock. Being tested along with the channel catfish were striped bass (*Morone saxatilis*), common carp (*Cyprinus carpio*), bluegill sunfish (*Lepomis macrochirus*), northern pike (*Esox lucius*), perch (*Perca* species), and redbelly tilapia (*Tilapia zillii*).

The channel catfish, along with striped bass and common carp, performed better than all the others. After only 12 trials the three species learned how to avoid getting the mild electric shock with a 50 percent success rate.

Learning How to Survive

The difference is attributed to the natural instinct of the species. For example, perch and redbelly tilapia tend to remain motionless in the face of danger, relying largely on their coloration to blend them into their surroundings and avoid the attentions of a predator. Striped bass and common carp, on the other hand, flee from danger. It is possible that they are genetically programmed to perform avoidance behavior. It is not clear if adult channel catfish also exhibit escape or avoidance behavior in the wild (although juveniles will swim away when threatened).

*⊕ A blue catfish (*Ictalurus furcatus*) displaying its nasal and chin barbels. The barbels are important in detecting food. Note the extremely wide mouth.*

Threatened North American Freshwater Catfish

Two species of *Ictalurus* face threats to their survival in the wild; two others may also be in danger, and one still needs to be evaluated. Eight *Noturus* species, the two *Prietella* species, the widemouth blindcat, and the toothless blindcat also face threats to their survival.

Common Name	Scientific Name	Official IUCN-UNEP Listing
Bagre del Panuco	*Ictalurus australis*	DD
Bagre Lobo	*I. lupus*	DD
Bagre de Rio Verde	*I. mexicanus*	VU
Yaqui catfish	*I. pricei*	VU
Bagre de Cuatro Ciénegas	*I.* spp.	NE
Smoky madtom	*Noturus baileyi*	CR
Yellowfin madtom	*N. flavipinnis*	VU
Carolina madtom	*N. furiosus*	DD
Orange madtom	*N. gilberti*	VU
Frecklebelly madtom	*N. minutus*	LR
Pygmy madtom	*N. stanauli*	VU
Caddo madtom	*N. taylori*	VU
Scioto madtom	*N. trautmani*	CR
	Prietella lundbergi	VU
Mexican blindcat	*P. phreatophila*	EN
Widemouth blindcat	*Satan eurystomus*	VU
Toothless blindcat	*Trogloglanis pattersoni*	VU

The symbols refer to the official categories listed by the World Conservation Union (IUCN-UNEP), which are explained in the glossary.

⊕ *Snake River in Grand Teton National Park is a typical habitat for freshwater catfish. The fish are found mainly on the muddy or sandy bottom of rivers.*

Commercial Fisheries

Several species of ictalurid catfish are reared commercially in the U.S. The main species is the channel catfish, although some fisheries concentrate on the blue catfish (*Ictalurus furcatus*), the white catfish, the yellow bullhead (*Ameiurus natalis*), the brown bullhead (*Ameiurus nebulosus*), and the flathead catfish. All have been introduced into areas outside their natural ranges for human consumption. The main center of production is Mississippi, but commercial production of the channel catfish began in 1910 in Kansas. Although the industry expanded from the outset, it took another 50 years before the most significant and spectacular surge in demand occurred. Catfish meat has continued to be popular among U.S. consumers ever since.

Most farming occurs in earthen ponds 40–80 inches (1–2 m) deep and around 5–20 acres (2–8 hectares) in area. Advanced techniques mean that yields as high as 35,300 pounds (16,000 kg) per 2.5 acres (1 ha) can be produced. Production is colossal, exceeding 250,000 tons (227,000 tonnes) per year. During the middle to late 1900s the U.S. catfish industry came under threat from foreign catfish imports from the Far East. The main challenge came from Vietnam and consisted of several species of shark catfish. It was estimated that imports stood at around 255 tons (226 tonnes) in 1998 but had risen to nearly 9,000 tons (8,200 tonnes) by 2001.

However, it would appear from the experiment that they are adequately equipped to learn to avoid danger by opting for an escape route.

Globetrotting Bullheads

The brown bullhead is perhaps the most "international" of the ictalurids and the best known of the bullheads. It is found outside its natural range in North America; New Zealand, and along with the black bullhead (*Ameiurus melas*) in many European countries, extending as far east as Russia.

Not all are welcome additions to the fish population. Bullheads are considered pests in many of their adoptive countries. Both the above species are large and predatory, and can therefore pose a serious threat to native species of fish, amphibians, and other aquatic life.

Catfish were first introduced into Europe in the last 30 years of the 19th century. There are records of bullheads being introduced into France in 1871 and records of specimens in the Seine River in 1879. Since then one or other of the two species has appeared in Austria, Belgium, the Czech Republic, Denmark, Great Britain, Germany, Hungary, Italy, The Netherlands, and the countries of the former Soviet Union. Elsewhere, populations are known from Chile, Mexico, and Puerto Rico.

By comparison, the channel catfish has been sparingly introduced outside North America, where it is widely distributed. Cyprus and Italy have established populations, and populations have recently been confirmed in Britain. There are no populations in Asian and African countries. However, populations in Brazil, Cuba, the Dominican Republic, Puerto Rico, and Hawaii have been successful.

Small but Fierce

The madtoms may be small, but what they lack in size they make up for in a very special way.

Like their group mates, the stonecats, madtoms have venom-producing cells at the base of their dorsal and pectoral fin spines. In humans the poison produces pain and symptoms similar to a bee sting. Also like bee stings, the reaction can be more severe in people who are allergic to the venom. However, the moderate toxicity neither kills nor seriously injures those attacked. It acts more as a deterrent to warn would-be predators that madtoms make a painful, distasteful, and unworthy mouthful.

Flat-headed Cats

Four species of ictalurids possess distinctive flat heads and, as previously mentioned, are generally referred to as flathead catfish. They are the Mexican blindcat and its close relative *Prietella lundbergi*, the flathead catfish, and the widemouth blindcat. The flathead catfish has normal pigmentation and eyes; the others are pinkish in color, and eyeless.

The flathead is also known as the yellow cat in reference to its body color, which ranges from yellowish to brown and is liberally mottled in black or brown, or the shovelhead catfish owing to its flat head and projecting lower jaw.

The flathead is highly cannibalistic but has itself been preyed on by humans for several centuries. Remains of flathead catfish are known from Native American middens (kitchen refuse dumps) dating back to around 1450. The locations of some of these middens fall outside the species' current distribution (central U.S. to eastern Mexico), indicating that flatheads were found in more northern regions in the past.

Blindcats

The Mexican blindcat (only described in 1995) and the widemouth blindcat, along with the unrelated toothless blindcat, are all found in subterranean waters such as wells and caves. All the species are pink, a common feature in animals that have evolved in dark, underground habitats. The pink coloration is a result of the flow of blood in the capillaries (small blood vessels) that can be seen under the white or uncolored skin and through the white muscle

Channel Catfish, Bullheads, and Their Relatives

The channel catfish has eight close relatives belonging to the same genus, *Ictalurus*. Of them three are considerably better known, particularly the blue catfish—a large species measuring around 5.4 feet (1.65 m). Among the bullheads the two best-known species are the brown bullhead and the black bullhead.

Common Name	Scientific Name	Approx. Size inches (cm)
Channel catfish	*Ictalurus punctatus*	52 (132)
Bagre del Panuco	*I. australis*	-
	I. balsanus	-
	I. dugesii	-
Blue catfish	*I. furcatus*	64 (165)
Headwater catfish or Bagre Lobo	*I. lupus*	18.9 (48)
Bagre de Rio Verde	*I. mexicanus*	-
	I. ochoterenai	-
Yaqui catfish	*I. pricei*	22.4 (57)
Snail bullhead	*Ameiurus brunneus*	11.4 (29)
White catfish	*A. catus*	37 (95)
Black bullhead	*A. melas*	26 (66)
Yellow bullhead	*A. natalis*	18.5 (47)
Brown bullhead	*A. nebulosus*	21.7 (55)
Flat bullhead	*A. platycephalus*	11.4 (29)
Spotted bullhead	*A. serracanthus*	11 (28)

tissues. Blindcats also lack eyes, another typical feature of cave-dwelling forms. Dark conditions favor the evolution of eyeless forms because in such habitats eyes are unnecessary and if present could be vulnerable to injury or infection.

Caves and other underground habitats tend to be fairly stable environments when left undisturbed. However, they are particularly susceptible to pollution through seepage and water-level fluctuations due to water extraction. Catfish living under such conditions face potential threats to their survival not shared by their relatives above ground.

Bagrid Catfish

Bagridae

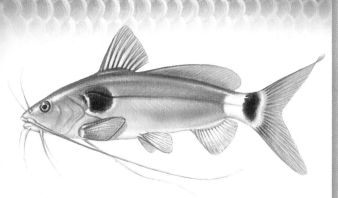

Two-spot pink bagrid (*Mystus micracanthus*)

Common name Bagrid catfish

Family Bagridae

Order Siluriformes

Number of species Around 210 in 30 genera

Size From 3.2 in (8 cm) to 6.6 ft (2 m)

Key features Widely ranging characteristics; common features are a dorsal fin with a spine at the front; pectoral fins with a spine; adipose fin; complete lateral line in most species; minimum number of barbels: 3 pairs—some species also possess an additional pair of nasal barbels; 2 pairs of nostrils widely separated from each other, with one exception (see main text)

Breeding Details only available for a few species, which care for their eggs and young (see main text)

Diet Extremely varied; includes plant material, snails, other invertebrates, fish, and even human feces

Habitat Estuaries, lakes, rivers, streams, and pools occupied by family overall; most confined to fresh water

Distribution Widely found in Asia and Africa

⊕ *The two-spot pink bagrid (*Mystus micracanthus*) is found in Sumatra, Java, Borneo, and Thailand, where it lives in shoals. It reaches 6 inches (15 cm) in length.*

In Africa there is a small, silvery catfish that feeds on worms and a giant catfish 13 times bigger that hunts fish. Yet both species are so closely related that they belong to the same genus.

BOTH THE CATFISH MENTIONED ABOVE, THE 6-inch (15-cm) long aluminum catfish (*Chrysichthys longipinnis*) from the Upper Congo River and the 6.6-ft (2-m) long and appropriately named *C. grandis* from Lake Tanganyika, would not at first sight appear to be close relatives. However, the relationship between the two species is based on similarities in the structure of certain bones, mainly around the eyes and ears, along with the thickness and plainness of their lips.

Such similarities, as well as others like the overall body profile, large head, jaws of differing lengths, and the nature of some of the barbels (all *Chrysichthys* have four pairs, with the nasal pair being short or very short) link not only these two species but also some 40 others.

Yet despite the similarities, there is also great variety within the genus. Some species, like the golden-yellow bodied *C. auratus* are very colorful and harmless. Others, like the mottled catfish or African wood cat (*C. ornatus*) can be dangerous to humans, since a puncture wound from its dorsal or pectoral fin spines may result in blood poisoning. The aptly named big-eyed miji catfish (*C. furcatus*) has unusually large eyes, and *C. sianenna* is a species often found diving down to depths of around 390 feet (120 m). The genus is equally diverse in terms of diet. Anything from vegetable matter to human feces can be found on the menu, and *C. helicophagus* feeds exclusively on snails.

A Question of Classification

The *Chrysichthys* catfish are so wide-ranging in terms of their size, characteristics, behavior, coloration, and feeding habits that it is difficult to accept that they are so closely related that

↑ *Chrysichthys stoppersii, one of the so-called aluminum cats—there are several similarly colored species—occurs exclusively in Lake Tanganyika, Africa. It feeds on crabs, worms, and carrion.*

they belong to a single genus. Apply the same thinking to the family as a whole, and it is easy to see why there is currently so much heated debate and difference of opinion.

Some experts believe that the Bagridae should be subdivided into seven subfamilies; some believe that there should be five subfamilies; others maintain that some of the genera actually belong to other families; and there is a group who says that the family should be divided into three separate families, some of them containing subfamilies! However, most authorities agree that the bagrid catfish represent the ancestral group from which many catfish families have subsequently evolved. In keeping with this belief, the present family, consisting of around 210 species, is difficult to describe in general terms.

Among the most significant characteristics

that most bagrids share is having a dorsal fin with a spine at the front. All species have an adipose fin. The pectoral fins are horizontal when they are extended and also have a spine. The lateral line runs the whole length of the body in nearly all species, and the minimum number of barbels is three pairs. Where a fourth pair is present, it usually consists of a short nasal (nose) pair. There are two pairs of nostrils that are widely separated in all genera except one (*Rita*). The front pair is located near the tip of the snout and the back pair closer to the eyes.

Many Questions

Even within this basic framework features vary enormously. For example, while all species have an adipose fin, it can be either very small or very large. The nostrils may or may not carry

⬆ *The tiny Guinea catfish (Mystus tengara), native to the Niger River in Africa, grows to just over 3 inches (8 cm) in length, yet still has room for a fourth pair of barbels on its "nose." This species makes a chirping sound as it spawns.*

nasal barbels. The dorsal fin usually has six to seven soft rays, but the number can rise to 20. The dorsal spine is either stout or weak and either serrated or smooth.

Many questions remain unanswered by the scientific authorities who try to classify the 210 or so species that make up the family Bagridae. For example, is having the adipose fin important enough to place all species within a single family? How significant is the presence or absence of the fourth pair of barbels? Do the form and number of teeth that are linked directly with the feeding habits play a central role in how the species should be subdivided? Scientists are still considering these and other questions. The future classification of the Bagridae is therefore set for major changes.

Varied Breeders

We do not know a great deal about the breeding behavior of bagrids. The limited information we have indicates that breeding strategies are extremely varied within the family. We know, for example, that *Bagrus docmak* grows to around 40 inches (1 m); males mature when they are three-quarters grown and

⊕ *Although it grows quite large, the giraffe catfish (Auchenoglanis occidentalis) is very popular as an aquarium fish. It has a peaceful nature and is tolerant of even small tankmates. It has a wide-ranging diet and does not compete aggressively for a particular food source.*

Milk-drinking Baby Bagrids

Various catfish, such as the long-tailed banjos (family Aspredinidae), *Pseudohemiodon*, *Loricariichthys,* and some plecos (family Loricariidae), care for their eggs and young more intensively than the majority of species in the order. Eggs may be carried around attached to the male or female, or the newborn fry may feed on nutrients secreted by the parent fish. In at least three species of bagrids egg and fry care show a combination of such techniques. It is possible that care also involves a modification or adaptation of the "milk secreting" ability seen in some of the talking catfish (family Doradidae), although this has not been proven.

In the long-whiskered catfish (*Mystus gulio*) females develop spongy, blood-rich belly tissue during breeding. In the shovelmouth catfish (*Aorichthys aor*) and the shovelnose catfish (*A. seenghala*) it is the males that develop the tissue, which extends to the undersides of the anal, pelvic, and caudal fins. While it is not known with certainty whether the eggs are actually incubated in this spongy tissue or in a nest, the latter appears to be the case.

During aquarium spawnings it has been reported that although males and young of shovelnose and shovelmouth catfish are commonly found in nests, "usually no eggs are seen." The young, however, have been found attached to the male shovelmouth catfish. They have also been noted to have consumed protein-rich, milky secretions produced by the male. In at least the shovelnose catfish the young are also reputed to feed exclusively on this body milk until they reach a size of around 1.8 inches (4.5 cm). It is not known whether this breeding strategy occurs in other bagrids, however.

⊕ *Black lancers (Bagrichthys hypselopterus) are natives of Sumatra. In the wild they are passive and lead solitary lives.*

females when they are a little over half their full size. We also know that this species produces white eggs.

The tawny dragon (*Pelteobagrus fluvidraco*) excavates a shallow nest in soft, fine-grained substrata during the summer. The male guards the eggs until they hatch some two days later. At least two *Chrysichthys* species excavate caves in river banks, lay their eggs inside, and then both parents guard them.

In the Guinea catfish (*Mystus tengara*) spawning among organic material in plant thickets is often accompanied by chirping sounds. Male black lancers (*Bagrichthys*

hypselopterus and *B. macracanthus*) produce an extended breeding tube or opening (the genital papilla) during the breeding season; the same applies to the harlequin lancer (*Bagroides melapterus*) and to various Asian bumblebees (*Leiocassis* species). However, details of actual spawning and egg care are lacking. In at least three species of bagrid, the long-whiskered catfish (*Mystus gulio*), the shovelmouth catfish (*Aorichthys aor*), and the shovelnose catfish (*A.seenghala*), egg and fry care go a significant stage further. They involve not just protection of the brood but nourishment of the newborn young (see box "Milk-drinking Baby Bagrids").

Although the red-tailed bagrid *(Mystus nemurus)* retains some of the coloration that gives rise to its common name, the hues tend to become progressively subdued with age.

Top Tank Bagrids

The 35 or so species belonging to the genus *Mystus* are the best known of all bagrids largely because several have been popular as aquarium fish for many years. Most of these bagrids are small or relatively small, between 3.2 and 14 inches (8–35 cm) in length, and so can be comfortably housed in moderate-sized aquariums. Some species, though, can grow quite large: The Asian red-tailed bagrid (*M. nemurus*) can grow to 24 inches (60 cm) long.

The attraction of *Mystus* species for aquarists lies in the relative ease with which many can be kept, as well as their interesting shapes, colors, or body patterns. They include the Asian red-tailed bagrid, the banded or pajama-striped bagrid (*M. vittatus),* and the gray catfish (*M. keletius*).

Bumblebees and Giraffes

The various Asian bumblebee catfish within the family are also popular. The fish have attractive body patterning consisting of irregular bands or blotches of dark and light coloration, which is vivid in the young, hence the name bumblebee. The bagrid "bees" can easily be told apart from their similar equivalents within the antenna catfish (family Pimelodidae) because *Leiocassis* species have a pair of nasal barbels, while their pimelodid cousins do not.

Perhaps a little surprisingly, owing to its large size of around 24 inches (60 cm), the giraffe catfish (*Auchenoglanis occidentalis*) can be listed among the bagrid aquarium favorites. It is simple to care for and becomes tame in captivity. So, too, does the red-tailed catfish (*Phractocephalus hemioliopterus*) of the family Pimelodidae.

Noisy Cats

Although the talking catfish (family Doradidae), the tandan catfish (family Plotosidae), and the squeakers (family Mochokidae) are the best-known vocalists among catfish, many bagrids also produce sounds.

For example, when stressed, Asian bumblebee catfish usually produce a noise that is often described as sounding like "kot" repeated several times over. Guinea catfish make a chirping sound during spawning, while *Auchenoglanis ngamensis*, a close relative of the giraffe catfish, emits grunts when it is removed from the water. The banded or pajama-striped bagrid, on the other hand, produces a buzzing sound, while the Amur dragon catfish (*Pelteobagrus brashnikowi*) generates gnashing sounds when it becomes excited.

Wels (*Silurus glanis*)

Common name Sheatfish

Family Siluridae

Order Siluriformes

Number of species Around 100 in 12 genera

Size From 1.8 in (4.5 cm) to maximum size of 16.4 ft (5 m)

Key features Body flattened from side to side from behind the head to the tail; 2 or 3 pairs of barbels, usually 2 on the lower jaw and 1 on the upper; lower jaw frequently slightly longer than the upper; short-based dorsal fin (7 rays or less) without a spine at the front; very long-based anal fin containing 41–110 rays; no adipose fin; pelvic fins sometimes absent

Breeding Depending on species, spawning takes place between June and August; nests may consist of depressions excavated by the male, which then guards the eggs until they hatch; some species undertake short migrations during floods

Diet Aquatic invertebrates, insects and other fish; larger species also feed on amphibians, waterfowl, and aquatic mammals such as voles

Habitat Large lakes, rivers, and backwaters; many inhabit turbid waters with sandy or muddy substrata; glass catfish prefer clean midwater zones where they collect in shoals; wels lives in brackish waters in the Baltic, Black and Caspian Seas—deeper waters with little current preferred, spending most of the day hiding under roots and overhangs

Distribution Widely distributed in Asia; 2 species occur in Europe

⊕ *The wels, or European catfish (Silurus glanis), is probably the best-known silurid; it is a fierce predator but very popular with anglers as a game and food fish.*

CATFISH

Sheatfish

Siluridae

Members of the sheatfish family, the silurids, display an impressive and varied range of sizes, shapes, and colors. Family resemblance only shows up in the way their fins and barbels are arranged.

MOST OF THE SHEATFISH FAMILY are found in Asia, but two species, the wels, or the European catfish (*Silurus glanis*), and Aristotle's catfish (*S. aristotelis*), are found in Europe. The wels is so widely known that the whole family is sometimes referred to as European catfish, although this is inaccurate.

Silurids look quite similar to the schilbeid catfish (family Schilbeidae), walking catfish (family Clariidae), and airsac catfish (family Heteropneustidae). However, they can be distinguished from other catfish families in several ways, although it is a combination of characteristics—rather than any single one—that makes identification quite easy (see box "Family Differences").

Silurids have no adipose fin and possess two or three pairs of barbels ("whiskers"); one or two pairs are situated on the lower jaw (known as mandibular barbels) with the other, often longer pair on the upper jaw (called maxillary barbels). The anal fin has a particularly long base, with as many as 110 rays in it, and it may join up with the caudal (tail) fin. In sharp contrast, the dorsal fin usually has seven or fewer rays, no spine, and is located well forward on the body.

Both Ends of the Scale

Despite the large number of species in the family, most of them are familiar only to catfish specialists or fishermen. The two species of silurids most recognizable to nonspecialists are the very distinctive glass catfish (*Kryptopterus bicirrhis*) and the wels or European catfish. The glass catfish grows to a maximum of 6 inches (15 cm); most specimens are in fact smaller. The wels, by contrast, is huge. Adult specimens

⊖ *The glass catfish (Kryptopterus bicirrhis), also known as the Asian glass catfish or the ghost or phantom glass catfish. Unlike other silurids, the glass catfish prefers to live in shoals, swimming in the flowing midwater currents rather than staying near the muddy river or lake beds.*

can often reach around 10 feet (3 m) in length and weigh over 440 pounds (200 kg). However, individuals measuring 16.4 feet (5 m) and weighing up to 675 pounds (305 kg) have also been recorded. Throughout the rest of the family there are many interesting species that

Family Differences

Some of the features that help distinguish sheatfish from their look-alike counterparts in other catfish families are summarized here. It is mostly a question of different fin characteristics.

Family Siluridae

Barbels	Two or three pairs
Dorsal fin	Short base; no spine
Adipose fin	Absent
Pelvic fins	Small, sometimes absent
Anal fin	Long base
Caudal fin	May be joined to anal fin

Family Schilbeidae

Barbels	Usually four pairs
Dorsal fin	Short base; spine present
Adipose fin	Usually present
Pelvic fins	Small, sometimes absent
Anal fin	Long base
Caudal fin	Not joined to anal fin

Family Clariidae

Barbels	Usually four pairs
Dorsal fin	Long base; no spine
Adipose fin	Absent
Pelvic fins	Small, sometimes absent
Anal fin	Long base
Caudal fin	Not joined to anal fin

Family Heteropneustidae

Barbels	Four pairs
Dorsal fin	Short base; no spine
Adipose fin	Absent or present as a low ridge
Pelvic fins	Small
Anal fin	Long base
Caudal fin	Not joined to anal fin

range in size from just 1.8 inches (4.5 cm) in the case of *Silurichthys sanguineus* to around 13 feet (4 m) in the case of Soldatov's catfish (*Silurus soldatovi*). Aristotle's catfish, found mostly in southern and western Greece, can grow to 6.6 feet (2 m) in length and can reach a weight of around 330 pounds (150 kg). However, around 50 percent of all silurid species are small fish measuring only about 12 inches (30 cm) or less.

Some of the medium-sized and larger species are caught on hook and line as game or sport fish, or are cultivated in ponds as food fish and to restock angling waters.

The Wels: Big Cat

The wels is the second largest and heaviest catfish in the world, surpassed only by the giant or Mekong catfish (*Pangasius gigas*). The wels has an appetite to match its size. Its main diet consists of bottom-living fish, but items as varied as crayfish, amphibians, and water voles also find their way onto its menu.

Because the wels is such a big, strong fish, it is a favorite among fishermen. It has been introduced to various European waters outside its native range, but some introductions have been more successful than others. During the 20th century wels introduced into Cyprus and Belgium failed to become established. However,

⊕ *The wels (Silurus glanis) has a voracious appetite, consuming almost anything it can swallow. It prefers to feed at night, but if there is food on offer, it will readily eat in the daytime as well.*

 SEE ALSO Catfish, Giant **37:42**

⊖ *An angler struggles to show off his enormous catch, a wels. The photograph illustrates clearly the size to which the powerful fish grow.*

attempts to introduce the fish to Britain, Spain, Italy, Denmark, the Netherlands, and elsewhere (both in the 19th and 20th centuries) appear to have proved more successful.

The first successful stocking in Britain seems to have occurred in 1880, when 70 small wels were released into a lake at Woburn Abbey in Bedfordshire, England. Most wels in Britain are probably descended from these few fish, although subsequent illegal imports and releases may well have added to current stocks. British wels differ from their counterparts in mainland Europe, particularly those introduced into the Rio Ebro in Spain, by their paler color

The Glass Cats Collection

The silurid genus *Kryptopterus* contains 17 species. Not all are glassily transparent, however, but even those that lack the characteristic have some silvery scales on the body. The most transparent members of the genus, in addition to *Kryptopterus bicirrhis*, are the smaller ghost or Asian glass catfish (*K. minor*), the Bornean glass catfish (*K. cryptopterus*), and the poor man's glass catfish (*K. macrocephalus*). There are also other "glass" catfish in the family, the most notable being *Ompok bimaculatus*—also, confusingly, called the glass catfish or Asian glass catfish, and Vaillant's butter catfish (*O. eugeniatus*).

Several members of the closely related Schilbeidae family are also known as glass catfish. The best-known of them are the African glass catfish or glass schilbeid (*Parailia pellucida*), the Congo catfish (*Ompok congica*), the West African glass catfish (*P. occidentalis*), and two species of *Pareutropius*—*P. debauwi* and *P. vanderweyeri*—both referred to (again, confusingly) as African glass catfish.

Schilbeid glass catfish can be easily distinguished from sheatfish glass catfish and other "glassy" family members. Schilbeids have a spine on their dorsal fin. Furthermore they usually have four pairs of barbels and an adipose fin. *Kryptopterus bicirrhis* and its close relatives have no spine on the dorsal fin, no adipose fin, and one or two pairs of barbels depending on the species.

⊖ *The Malayan glass catfish, or Vaillant's butter catfish (Ompok eugeniatus) is characterized by two spots—one behind the eye and one behind the gill cover.*

and much smaller size. The color difference is attributed to the murky waters where they are found, and the size variation to the lower temperatures and shorter summers typical of Britain. An average British wels weighs about 30 pounds (13.6 kg), compared with those recorded in waters in more southern locations such as the Ebro, where reports of individuals weighing over 200 pounds (90 kg) are common. Although still well below the weight attained by specimens in native waters, it is believed that some may eventually match the size of their genuinely native cousins, especially since the species lifespan is around 80 years.

Pond Breeding

In some European countries the wels is bred commercially for human consumption as well as for stocking angling waters. Several methods are used, the most common employing two or four stages respectively. The two-stage technique involves introducing several pairs of brood fish into a pond measuring about 0.25 acres (0.1 ha) and then supplying each pair with a nest constructed out of willow or alder roots. The ponds also contain carp, a food supply for the wels.

Once the catfish fry reach a size of around 2 inches (5 cm), they are transferred to larger rearing ponds, again containing small carp. The young catfish feed on a range of live foods, including insects and carp. After one summer they can reach a weight of up to 7 oz (200 g). With plenty of young carp to eat, the young catfish can more than quadruple their size, reaching a weight of around 2.2 pounds (1 kg) after a second summer. Wels mature at around four years of age.

In the four-stage method individual pairs of wels are placed in small ponds, each with an artificial willow and alder-root nest. Once the eggs have been laid, the nests are transferred to hatching basins. After hatching, which takes about three days, the fry are left in the basins for a further nine or ten days and are then transferred to rearing ponds containing a rich supply of live foods. After a further three to five weeks they are then transferred to the final rearing ponds measuring 0.25 to 0.5 acres (0.1–0.2 ha), where they are intensively fed until the end of the summer, when the first harvests are taken.

The wels' breeding season starts with pairs forming in spring or early summer depending on the location. In Europe's more southern regions, spawning starts in May or June. Farther north, spawning starts a little later in June and continues into August. Generally, spawning occurs in shallow water, and up to 500,000 eggs may be laid by a large female, but 100,000 is probably more common. Hatching takes about 3 days (one report, though, refers to an incubation period of 3 weeks). The male guards the eggs until they hatch.

Glass Catfish

Surprising though it may seem, the huge, solid wels is a close relative of the tiny, delicate, ethereal glass catfish. Apart from the obvious differences in appearance and geographical distribution between the species, they also differ in their behavior, most notably in the fact that the glass catfish, along with its closest relatives, forms shoals.

A single glass catfish is a pretty sight, but not a memorable one. However, a shoal of several hundred individuals hovering in midwater creates a unique visual impression that once seen is never forgotten. As their bodies tilt at an angle toward the surface, the light catches the beautifully delicate skeletons and shines right through the transparent flesh, and the silvery body sacs shimmer in the sunlight.

Transparent Qualities

Such a sparkling display is quite a remarkable achievement for a fish whose body muscles lack any color at all. The little color that the species has comes instead from the bones of the ribs, vertebral column, fin rays, and skull, the eyes, and the blood of the gills showing through the gill covers, along the ribs, and below the backbone. All this is augmented by the silvery body sac that contains the internal organs and a few scattered melanophores, or pigment-containing cells, on the body.

The glass catfish is an inoffensive species that shuns the bottom-dwelling lifestyle shown by most other members of the family. It prefers to spend its time in midwater facing the current. At first glance this would seem to be the perfect recipe for disaster: a small, harmless, defenseless fish choosing to live in full view of potential predators. Yet, despite this apparent exposure, the glass catfish survives in substantial numbers in the wild. It has been suggested that the mirrorlike surface of the body sac, which is largely confined to a small, almost spherical mass just behind and below the head, reflects the colors of the fish's surroundings, allowing it to blend into the background and become more difficult for a predator to target.

Disguise or Display?

This theory is open to debate, however, because as glass catfish move, the same mirrorlike qualities that may provide them with protective camouflage actually reflect sunlight, possibly pinpointing their position more accurately for would-be predators.

Then, of course, there is the skeleton itself, which is perfectly visible irrespective of the reflective qualities of the body sac. Perhaps it is the confusion created by a shoal of fish whose individual body outline is difficult to make out and whose reflective body sacs flash in the sunlight, allied to the "safety in numbers" principle, that make the species so successful.

⊕ *Like other glass catfish, the giant glass catfish (Kryptopterus species) has an elongate, laterally compressed body and long sensory barbels.*

Common name
Schilbeid catfish

Common name Schilbeid catfish

Family Schilbeidae (Schilbidae)

Order Siluriformes

Number of species Around 45 to 60 in around 18 genera

Size Range from 3.2 in (8 cm) to 19.7 in (50 cm)

Key features Extremely varied; most have a forked tail, a long or moderately long anal fin, and 4 pairs of barbels; some have translucent or almost-transparent bodies, with or without dorsal, adipose, or pelvic fins

Breeding Few details available; huge numbers of tiny eggs produced; no parental care is known to occur; spawning may involve migration during flood, then mating in shallow or swampy areas

Diet Primarily animal matter, from terrestrial insects and aquatic invertebrates to fish

Habitat Usually found in midwater; the butter catfish or grass cutter close to the bottom; water often prone to seasonal flooding—at such times the catfish are found in shallow and swampy areas

Distribution Approximately 75 percent in tropical regions of Africa; the remainder mainly in southern Asia

The 14-inch (35.5-cm) grass cutter, butter, or striped catfish (Schilbe mystus), a species native to Africa that is bred for the aquarium and as a food fish.

CATFISH

Schilbeid Catfish Schilbeidae

The schilbeids are extremely confusing catfish: Some look like sheatfish, some look like shark catfish, and others resemble bagrid catfish.

IT IS EXTREMELY HARD TO DESCRIBE a schilbeid. If all the 45 to 60 or so species in the family had the same, or even similar, characteristics, it would be relatively easy, but that is not the case with these catfish. A closer examination of the features associated with schilbeid catfish helps explain why.

Loose Connections

First, let us consider fins. Dorsal fins are present in some species but absent in others. If a dorsal fin is present, it may have either a stout spine or a weak one. Some species have an adipose fin. In other species the adipose fin may be present during the juvenile stages but disappears gradually with age. Furthermore, the fish may or may not have pelvic fins.

Body shape is also extremely varied. In some species the chest and belly may be shaped like a keel. The nostrils may be close together or far apart. Other features vary just as much, making it very difficult to pinpoint the salient features of a schilbeid. However, there are a few characteristics that nearly all species share. When they occur in conjunction with a combination of the features listed above, the fish concerned is likely to belong to the family Schilbeidae.

Because of their varied characteristics there is some uncertainty regarding the validity of the family itself and how close it is to its nearest relatives. Some scientists believe that the schilbeids and the shark catfish (family Pangasiidae) are

The African glass catfish (Pareutropius debauwi) is an unusually patterned species found in the Congo and Gabon regions of Africa. It grows to about 3 inches (8 cm) in length.

 SEE ALSO Catfish, Bagrid **37**:22; Sheatfish **37**:30; Catfish, Shark **37**:42

so close to each other that they should be thought of as subfamilies of a single family. Other taxonomists note that schilbeids can be confused with sheatfish or glass catfish in the family Siluridae, but believe that although many schilbeids behave in a way similar to the glass catfish, these similarities are superficial and do not make a sufficiently strong case for including them all in the same family. Yet others believe that schilbeids are close to the bagrid catfish (family Bagridae). Until the taxonomic questions are fully resolved, it is convenient to assign the schilbeids to their own family.

Adopting this approach, two groups can be identified within the family. One, containing perhaps around 75 percent of all the species—although not of all the genera—occurs in Africa; the remainder are Asian species.

Farther down the classification level some authorities subdivide the genera into subgenera. For example, the glass catfish of the genus *Parailia* are frequently subdivided into two subgenera, *Parailia* and *Physailia*, in which case a species like the Congo glass catfish becomes *Parailia (Parailia) congica*, while the West African glass catfish becomes *Parailia (Physailia) occidentalis*; similarly, the genus *Schilbe* may be divided into two subgenera, *Schilbe* and *Eutropius*.

→ *The Congo glass catfish (*Parailia congica*), one of three species of African glass catfish and a popular aquarium choice. It is the only African glass fish that does not have an adipose fin.*

Best-known Africans

Most of the best-known species are African in origin, probably because they have been more widely available as aquarium fish than their Asian relatives. Of all the schilbeid species, those that are most frequently seen outside the scientific community are the various glass catfish (*Parailia* and *Pareutropius* species) and the *Schilbe* catfish.

The three best-known African glass cats are the African glass catfish (*Parailia pellucida*), the West African glass catfish (*P. occidentalis*), and the less transparent Congo glass catfish (*P. congica*). The Congo glass catfish lacks an adipose fin, and all three lack a dorsal fin.

The barbels are particularly long in all *Parailia* species, and this feature, added to the overall transparency that makes the skeleton visible through the flesh, plus their habit of swimming in shoals in midwater, means that the fish can be very easily confused with the Asian glass catfish (*Kryptopterus bicirrhis*).

Not So Transparent

Two rather less "glassy" species, the so-called Debauwi glass catfish (*Pareutropius debauwi* and *P. vanderweyeri*), are confusingly referred to quite frequently as African glass catfish, although *P. debauwi* is also referred to as the candy-striped catfish. The species have also become relatively well known, but only since the 1990s, although the former was first imported into Europe for aquariums as long ago as 1954. The two species are very similar to each other, but *P. vanderweyeri* has black streaks on both lobes of the caudal fin.

Record-breaking Schilbeid?

Information regarding the breeding of schilbeid catfish is scarce, hard to come by, and inconsistent. One particular aspect of reproduction may be well known, while there may be little or no data regarding another. For example, it is known that certain species, such as the grass cutter or butter catfish, are fixed-season spawners. They breed only once a year during the floods. It is also known that this species, along with others, such as one of the relatives of the glass catfish (*Parailia spiniserratus*), move upriver to spawn in shallow areas during the periods of flood. As for the Debauwi glass catfish, we do not know if they migrate or not, but we do know that they lay adhesive (sticky) eggs. No parental care has been reported.

Perhaps the most amazing fact we have concerning schilbeid reproduction relates to the number of eggs produced by *Schilbe mandibularis* from the Gold Coast of Africa. Females have been found to contain eggs all of the same size, indicating that the species is a once-a-year spawner. What is remarkable, though, is that a female weighing no more than 3.5 oz (100 gm) can produce and carry as many as 17,600 tiny eggs, each measuring about 0.03 inch (0.075 cm) in diameter.

and so is not such an important food fish but an admirable aquarium species.

Best-known Asians

By far the best-known Asian schilbeid is the false Siamese shark (*Platytropius siamensis*). The "false" part of the name defers to the "true" Siamese shark catfish or iridescent shark (*Pangasius hypophthalmus*). The false Siamese shark is a beautiful species with long, elegant barbels and a silvery, highly reflective grayish sheen all over its body. It is not exploited as a food fish, probably because it only grows to around 10 inches (25 cm), whereas its much larger look-alike grows up to 51 inches (130 cm) and a weight of some 35 pounds (16 kg), making it a more viable product.

Some way behind the false Siamese shark in the popularity stakes is yet another "glass" catfish, the 3.2 inch (8 cm) long striped glass catfish (*Pseudeutropius atherinoides*). Although known to science since 1794, this delightful little fish has only become widespread outside its natural Indian range since the 1990s.

Fish for Eating

Some *Schilbe* species are also relatively well known, particularly the grass cutter or butter catfish (*Schilbe mystus*) and the African shoulder-spot catfish (*S. marmoratus*). The grass cutter is popular not just as an aquarium fish (the main reason for its worldwide fame) but because it is also a tasty food fish. Although not especially big at around 14 inches (35 cm), it is large enough to have become important in local commercial fisheries.

The African shoulder-spot catfish is much smaller—around 6.3 inches (16 cm) in length—

⊕ *Pareutropius longifilis* **is a tiny African glass catfish only 3.5 inches (9 cm) long that comes from the fast-flowing rivers of East Africa.**

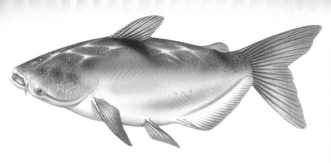

Giant catfish (*Pangasius gigas*)

Common name Shark catfish

Family Pangasiidae

Order Siluriformes

Number of species Around 25 in 2 genera

Size From 9 in (23 cm) to 10 ft (3 m)

Key features Elongated body; flattish head; soft skin; large eyes—set very low on head in giant catfish; 2 to 3 pairs of barbels, often quite small, nasal barbels absent; well-formed dorsal fin with 1 prominent spine and 1 very small spine; small adipose fin; strong caudal fin; pectoral fins with prominent spine; anal fin contains 26–46 rays

Breeding Many seasonal, though breeding season may vary even within the same species, depending on location; some are nonseasonal spawners

Diet Most have a wide-ranging diet that includes both animals and plants; the giant catfish is totally herbivorous

Habitat Large watercourses and lakes

Distribution Southern Asia from Borneo to Pakistan

Status Giant catfish rated as Endangered by IUCN-UNEP (World Conservation Union); not listed by CITES

⊕ *The giant or Mekong catfish (Pangasius gigas) is a species native to the Mekong River system. A popular food fish, it can grow to 10 feet (3 m) in length.*

Shark Catfish
Pangasiidae

The rivers of southern Asia are home to a number of catfish species that could, with some imagination, be mistaken for sharks. They are the 25 pangasiids commonly referred to as the shark catfish.

LOOK AT THE UNDULATING SWIMMING movements of these catfish, together with their smooth skins, long bodies, and prominent dorsal fins, and it is not hard to see why the Pangasiidae are usually referred to as shark catfish—even though they are not remotely related to true sharks.

Depending on which classification is used, there are between 21 and 29 species of shark catfish. Formerly, the family contained at least five separate genera. However, following an important review of the family in 1991, plus the description of two new species, one in 1999 (*Pangasius sanitwongsei*) and another in 2000 (*P. djambal*), it is now generally accepted that there are only two genera within the family: *Pangasius* with 22 species and *Helicophagus* with two or maybe three species.

Both genera are quite similar. One of the most significant differences is the presence of teeth in the roof of the mouth (the palatine bone) in *Pangasius* and their absence in *Helicophagus*. In *Pangasius* some of the jaw teeth disappear with age, but they are retained in *Helicophagus*. There are also other differences, some relating to the position of the eye and nostrils and the disappearance of barbels as fish age, but the tooth arrangement is probably the best distinguishing feature.

Iridescent Shark
Any species that contains the word "shark" as part of its name immediately raises interest among fish enthusiasts. Such is the case with the iridescent shark (*Pangasius hypophthalmus*), young specimens of which, in addition, have two beautiful reflective (iridescent) bands running the length of the body from behind the head to the tail. Not surprisingly, therefore, this

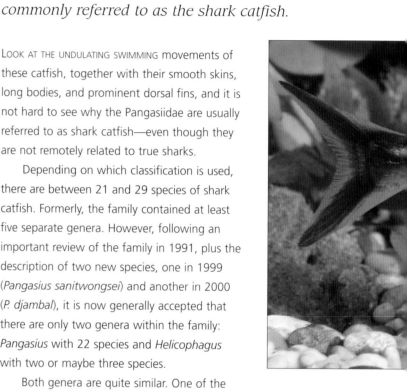

⊕ *The iridescent shark (Pangasius hypophthalmus), showing the reflective longitudinal bands that give the species one of its common names. It is found mainly in large rivers in Southeast Asia, where it forms shoals.*

⊖ *The golden tiger shark catfish is a variety of the iridescent shark.*

species has been popular with fishkeepers ever since the first specimens arrived from Asia during the 1960s.

In 1937 the iridescent shark was renamed *P. sutchi*, replacing the name *P. hypophthalmus* given to the species in 1878. Things remained that way for another 54 years, until the review of 1991 concluded that the name should revert to the 1878 version—*P. hypophthalmus*. Although this is now the valid name for the species, it is still widely referred to as *P. sutchi*.

Popular Food Fish

The iridescent shark is one of several catfish species harvested or cultivated in large quantities as food fish in Asia. Along with walking catfish (family Clariidae) it accounts for the bulk of an annual crop of nearly 290 million pounds (130,000 metric tonnes). Its popularity as a food fish is such that it has been introduced for this purpose into several regions outside its natural range, including the Philippines, Indonesia, and Singapore. Some populations have now become established in the wild in Singapore and, possibly, the Philippines. Cultivation of this species also occurs elsewhere but on a more modest scale.

Generally speaking, captive breeding involves the use of hormonal injections—a common and effective technique used on many other cultivated fish species. This results in large numbers of fertilized eggs, which are then hatched and reared either in ponds or in floating cages in rivers.

While undoubtedly being the top-selling pangasiid catfish, other family members are also sought out as food fish. Two species in particular are worth mentioning: the paroon shark (*P. sanitwongsei*) and *P. djambal*, known locally as "trey pra." The paroon shark is the less important of the two because in some areas its meat is considered of lower quality than that of its relatives, including the iridescent shark. This belief arises from the species' scavenging habits, which include, according to local rumor, a liking for dead dogs. (Drowned dogs are common in the wet season.)

Trey pra has top-quality white meat that is

⊕ *The paroon shark or giant pangasius (Pangasius sanitwongsei) is one of the largest of all freshwater fish, with specimens sometimes reaching 10 feet (3 m) in length.*

Catfish Wars

Owing to their size, abundance, the ease with which they can be bred and reared in captivity, as well as the quality of their meat, several species of shark catfish are important food fish. In the past most of the consumption of shark catfish meat was confined to Asia. However, as breeding and rearing methods have improved, exports have increased correspondingly. As a result, a situation is now developing that has major implications for catfish farmers outside the region, particularly in the U.S. Here the main catfish-breeding centers are in southern states like Louisiana, Arkansas, and Mississippi, with smaller quantities produced in Florida.

The main species cultured in these states are channel catfish (predominantly *Ictalurus punctatus* of the family Ictaluridae), but the iridescent shark is also reared. In Asia the main species are walking catfish (*Clarias* species of the family Clariidae) and various shark catfish. Of the latter the most important species is the iridescent shark, but others, most notably the paroon shark and (since 2000) *P. djambal*, are all quite significant. It is not clear which of the above species are regarded as presenting the greatest threat to U.S. catfish producers, but it seems that the two most likely candidates are walking catfish and the iridescent shark.

Figures quoted for U.S. catfish imports from Vietnam in recent years show a dramatic increase: In 1998 U.S. catfish producers estimated that 575,000 pounds (260 metric tonnes) of catfish were imported; by 2000–2001 the figure had soared to around 20 million pounds (more than 9,000 metric tonnes). Quite clearly, U.S. catfish breeders are facing a growing challenge from the East, one that is being tackled in a campaign that some are calling a "Catfish War."

considered superior to the yellowish meat of the iridescent shark. It can also be induced to breed throughout the year and is prolific: 300,000 larvae were produced at two farms during 2000 as part of the European Union-backed Catfish Asia Project that is being undertaken by European and Vietnamese research centers.

Cat of Many Names

The iridescent shark's ongoing popularity is reflected in the array of common names by which the species is known. In addition to iridescent shark, there are at least nine others: iridescent shark catfish, Siamese shark, candy-striped catfish, sutchi catfish (a name used by the Food and Agriculture Organization), Thailand catfish (a name used in Taiwan rather than Thailand), silver catfish, sharkfin catfish, Swai (a name used by the American Fisheries Society), and Asian shark catfish (rather an unhelpful name, since all shark catfish come from Asia).

The iridescent shark can grow to just over 51 inches (130 cm) in length, but it tends to remain smaller in captivity. As a result, it is possible to keep this fish in moderately sized aquariums. The fish also has remarkable resilience and hardiness, so it is easy to see why it has been popular with fish fanciers for so long. Nowadays aquarium technology, commercial foods, and husbandry techniques have advanced to such an extent that it is easier than before to cater to the needs of this and other large species of fish. The iridescent shark is set to remain popular for many years to come.

Giant Catfish

The toothless vegetarian giant catfish from the Mekong River is an intriguing species. It is both sacred and hunted, and its young have not been seen in the wild since the day the fish was officially described back in 1930. For a species that has been fished regularly as part of local culture, and whose migratory route and timing are firmly established, there is remarkably little hard information about the biology of the giant catfish. Even its scientific name has been a matter of some confusion. It was only in 1991 that the status of the genus *Pangasianodon* (whose only species was *P. gigas*) was reassessed, with the result that *Pangasianodon* was absorbed into the genus *Pangasius*. As well as its common name of giant catfish the species is also known as the Mekong catfish and the Thailand giant catfish.

Missing Parts

Two features set the giant catfish apart from its nearest relatives: the lack of teeth and the absence of barbels on the lower jaw. However, although these features are characteristics of adult specimens, we cannot say for sure if young, or even medium-sized, giant catfish also display them, because no subadult specimens have ever been examined. We do know, however, that in at least some of the giant catfish's relatives the teeth gradually disappear

⊖ *A Vietnamese fisherman tries his luck on the Mekong River in Thailand, casting a net to catch a wild giant catfish. The fish—which can reach a weight of 660 pounds (300 kg)— faces an uncertain future in its native waters, which extend through Laos, Cambodia, Thailand, Vietnam, and possibly also part of China.*

Festival Food and Oil

Giant catfish have traditionally been associated with Thai New Year festivities, which, in the past, lasted for up to three weeks during April and May. Coincidentally, this is the time when the flesh of the giant catfish is at its tastiest, since the fish have used up much of their body fat during their upstream spawning migrations.

Perhaps even more important than the actual flavor of the flesh is the belief that eating giant catfish, or *Pla Buek*, as it is known locally, leads to a long, healthy, and prosperous life. Add the two important ingredients of excellent eating and life-enhancing qualities together, and it is easy to understand why prime giant catfish meat commands equally prime prices in Thailand.

Pla Buek has also been fished over the years for its oil. Large fish, which regularly weigh well over 220 pounds (100 kg), yield correspondingly large quantities of the oil. It makes extraction a worthwhile exercise, despite the fact that wild population levels are low and that the fist-sized stones sometimes found in the stomachs of the giant catfish (perhaps accidentally swallowed while feeding) can wreak havoc with oil-extraction machinery.

with age, and it is possible that the same applies to the giant catfish.

Similarly, it is necessary to examine juvenile giant catfish, as well as a series of progressively older specimens, in order to determine whether or not barbels have been present at earlier stages in the fish's life. For example, it has been suggested that barbels may indeed be present even in adult specimens, but that they are overgrown by flesh as the jaws become progressively fatter with advancing age.

Some doubts therefore exist about the biology of the giant catfish, a situation likely to remain unresolved for some time in view of the much-reduced numbers of the species currently believed to exist in the wild. It is more likely, though, that the answers to these and other outstanding questions may be provided by

studies being carried out on captive-bred stocks currently being cultured for reintroduction into some of the giant catfish's traditional waters. Captive-bred specimens in which spawning has been induced by means of hormone injections have yielded, on average, 17.6–22 pounds (8–10 kg) of eggs. For wild species the breeding seasons starts with an upriver migration of several thousand miles between mid-April and the end of May, possibly reaching as far north as Lake Tali in Yunnan, China.

Threats to Survival

Because so little is known about the life of the giant catfish, it is impossible to say with any certainty what influence environmental factors may have had on populations of the species in the wild.

One thing that is definitely known, however, is that intense fishing over many years brought the species to the brink of extinction. Today the situation may be a little more hopeful, particularly as a result of the release of thousands of young fish from captive breeding programs into rivers inhabited by giant catfish. It is hoped that the released fish will become established and help sustain the existing populations.

Gradually, an expanding database relating to this largest of all catfish is beginning to emerge. With luck, as we learn more about the fish, and as the release of captive-bred specimens and control of the various fisheries begin to have an effect, Pangasius gigas will once again begin to enjoy the prospects of a brighter future.

Clown catfish (*Gagata cenia*)

Common name Asian hillstream catfish

Family   Sisoridae (Bagariidae)

Order   Siluriformes

Number of species Around 100 in around 20 genera

Size   From 0.8 in (2 cm) to around 8.2 ft (2.5 m)

Key features Generally flattened or conical head; 4 pairs of
barbels (except the whiptail, which has 6 pairs);
mouth underslung; dorsal fin with short base
placed well forward, with the front edge in front
of body midline; dorsal fin often carries a spine;
adipose fin present; skin often quite thick and
granular; chest and belly area flattened; may
possess chest, belly, mouth, lip, or fin
modifications for clinging to surfaces

Breeding   No details available

Diet   Most feed off encrusting algae and the
microfauna they shelter; the giant river catfish
(*Bagarius yarelli*) and closest relatives feed on
prawns, invertebrates, and fish

Habitat   Flowing waters in mountain rivers and streams,
including torrents; usually found in areas with
gravel, pebble, rock, or boulder substrata and
at altitudes to over 4,900 ft (1,500 m)

Distribution Widely in southern Asia from Syria and Turkey
eastward as far as southern China and Borneo

*① The bottom-dwelling clown catfish (*Gagata cenia*) is about
6 inches (15 cm) long. One of the six species in its genus, it is
found in India, Myanmar, and Thailand.*

Asian Hillstream Catfish

Sisoridae

*In the wild, sisorids are adventurous, taking their
chances against raging torrents; yet some of them
have also found a more restful niche as aquarium fish.*

THE TINY INDIAN CATFISH KNOWN as the dwarf
anchor catfish (*Hara jerdoni*) is smaller than a
thumbprint; yet this "micro" catfish, more than
any other member of its family (Sisoridae), has
been responsible for the huge growth of
interest in the varied and fascinating Asian
hillstream catfish, especially in Europe.

Micro Cats with Mega Influence

It all began in the 1990s. Initially, it was
assumed that the beautiful little specimens of
the dwarf anchor catfish were babies. They
were not; they were fully mature representatives
of their species. European aquarium keepers
found them irresistible; indeed, the sight of a
shoal of minuscule dwarf anchors scuttling
around the bottom of an aquarium is
unforgettable.

Interest then spread to their closest
relatives, and soon species such as the equally
tiny elongated moth catfish (*H. horai*), the
slightly larger butterfly catfish (*H. hara*), and the
much larger giant moth catfish (*H. filamentosa*)
that grows to the substantial size—in *Hara*
terms—of 4 inches (10 cm) found homes in
European aquariums. Members of the genus
Hara were closely followed by representatives of
the genus *Gagata*, including the slender, black
and silvery clown catfish (*Gagata cenia*). Clown
catfish have the added bonus—from an
aquarium keeper's point of view—of sometimes
occurring in an albino form with a white-pink
body and pink-red eyes. A third genus, *Laguvia*,
also produced an attractive aquarium species,
the splendidly mottled cheetah catfish (*Laguvia
shawi*), which is slightly larger than its dwarf
anchor cousin.

*⊕ The butterfly catfish
(Hara hara) from India is
2 in (5cm) long, making
it more than twice the
size of the pioneering
dwarf anchor catfish,
the first of the Asian
hillstream catfish to
become popular with
aquarists.*

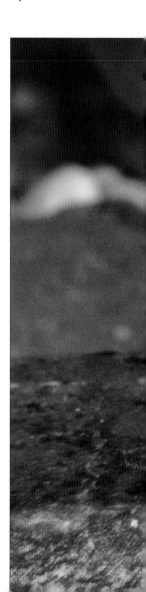

Sisor—the Atypical Sisorid

The family Sisoridae was created in honor of the whiptail catfish (*Sisor rhabdophorus*), a species that has a whiplike extension of the top of the caudal (tail) fin but is not related to the whiptail catfish of the family Loricariidae. Yet despite having a whole family named after it, the single species of *Sisor* is not a typical sisorid catfish—at least, not in several important respects.

All sisorids have four pairs of barbels. However, the whiptail has six pairs of barbels. There is one pair of maxillary (upper jaw) barbels and no fewer than five pairs of mandibular (lower jaw) barbels. The supplementary barbels on the lower jaw are the result of the outer mandibular barbels splitting close to their base. All hillstream catfish also have a dorsal fin, which in most species carries a spine. However, there is no spine on the dorsal fin of the whiptail catfish. Furthermore, all species possess an adipose fin, although in the whiptail catfish it is reduced to a single spine.

Staying Put

As their name indicates, wild Asian hillstream catfish tend to live in fast-flowing stretches of mountain water courses. All species live on the bottom, clear of the main force of the water flow (which is why aquarium species like to congregate on the floor of the tank). Nevertheless, faced with the permanent challenge of how best to avoid being swept away, most members of the family have evolved mechanisms to help them cling to rocks, boulders, or pebbles. Many have also evolved distinctive, wedgelike head shapes designed to make the flowing water press the fish down onto the stream bottom as it passes over them.

Sticky Solutions

Faced with the challenge of keeping on the bottom in the fast-flowing waters, sisorids have come up with some fascinating solutions. The various *Hara* species mentioned are, for

→ *The Indian catfish (Gagata schmidti) is about 2.8 inches (7 cm) long. Despite the common name, it is found in Sumatra.*

Fast-lane Gills

In some of the closer relatives of *Glyptosternon,* although not those in the genus *Glyptosternon* itself, an interesting adaptation to living in the "fast lane" of torrential waters has evolved. The adaptation, a modification to the gills, does not increase the fishes' sticking ability but is a direct consequence of living under such conditions.

In most fish species the gill openings extend onto the lower surface of the head, increasing the area available for absorbing oxygen from the water. However, in species that spend most of their life pressed against the bottom, such an arrangement is unnecessary because little water passes under the head. Consequently, for fish living in such environments, the lower part of the gill apparatus becomes redundant and may end up disappearing altogether.

This is what has happened in six of the genera that form the subfamily Glyptosterninae. In these fish the gill openings have become much smaller and are now restricted to the sides and upper part of the head. In other words, to areas that receive the full force of the water current. While such a decrease in oxygen-absorbing tissue might prove fatal for fish living in gentler environments, it is perfect for torrent-loving species. The higher oxygen content of the fast-flowing water means there is no risk of running short despite the reduced gill apertures; it is a case of quality rather than quantity.

example, sometimes referred to as belly sucker catfish, while species in the *Nangra* genus are known as broad-headed catfish, and *Laguvia* species are collectively referred to as flat-headed catfish. The names point to the various features that help these fish remain adhered to the bottom with minimum effort on their part.

Species in the genus *Pseudecheneis* display several bottom-hugging modifications. For example, in *Pseudecheneis sulcatus* a large part of the thoracic (chest) area of the body, from just behind the mouth almost to the front edge of the belly, is wrinkled and bears tiny hooks. It forms a large, efficient suction pad. A similar chest sucker arrangement is found in the belly sucker fish (*Glyptothorax coheni*) and other members of the genus *Glyptothorax,* as well as in species of the *Hara* genus, which are also, confusingly, known as belly sucker fish.

In other *Pseudecheneis* species the function is taken over either by expanded fins and their rays or by the fins and lips together. In species in which the fins are the only means of "sticking around," the pectoral and pelvic fins often overlap each other. In such cases the soft

rays that are closest to the body are used to pump out any water that seeps into the space under the body of the fish. This creates a region of low pressure, something like a vacuum, which helps keep the body of the fish pressed securely against the bottom. The genera *Coraglanis, Euchiloglanis, Exostoma, Glyptosternon,* and others all use one or other of the above lip and fin solutions to prevent being swept away..

Three-way Split

Although they do share certain common features, Asian hillstream catfish present an assortment of shapes and sizes. Numerous differences exist in almost every body feature, from the distance between the nostrils, the presence or absence of teeth, to the type of (or lack of) suction mechanism.

Some scientists believe that the differences can be used to distinguish three separate subfamilies (see box "Three Controversial Subfamilies"), although the subdivisions are not hugely significant to people outside the scientific community.

Three Controversial Subfamilies

Some experts believe that there are sufficient "collections" of similarities for the various sisorid genera to be grouped into three subfamilies: the Sisorinae, the Bagarinae, and the Glyptosterninae.

The first subfamily, the Sisorinae, contains the whiptail catfish. Its singularly different characteristics place the whiptail catfish apart from other hillstream catfish (see box "*Sisor*—the Atypical Sisorid.")

The Bagarinae groups together fish that do not have the series of bony plates that the whiptail has between the dorsal and caudal fin. In addition, members of the subfamily have a strong first ray in the pectoral and pelvic fins. The group includes all the best-known species and genera, such as the giant river catfish (*Bagarius yarelli*), the clown catfish, the dwarf anchor catfish, the belly sucker catfish, the cheetah catfish, and all their relatives.

The Glyptosterninae do not have bony plates between the dorsal and caudal fin either, but can be distinguished from the Bagarinae in that the first pectoral and pelvic rays are soft and weak.

Walking catfish (*Clarias batrachus*)

Common name Walking catfish

Family Clariidae

Order Siluriformes

Number of species 100 in around 13 genera

Size From 4.7 in (12 cm) to around 4.6 ft (1.4 m)

Key features Elongated body, with some species eel-like; dorsal and anal fins long-based and lack a spine at the front—these fins may be joined to the caudal fin or may be separate; adipose fin usually absent; pectoral fins usually have spine (used in walking), but both pectoral and pelvic fins may be absent; body scaleless; head often flattened and covered in bony plates; eyes range from well formed to tiny or absent; mouth terminal (located at the tip of the snout) with 4 pairs of long barbels in most species (3 in some); modified gills and arborescent and superbranchial organs present in most genera to allow fish to breathe out of water

Breeding Usually at night, at beginning of rainy season, in shallow water; nesting possible but the eggs left unprotected once spawning completed; hatching around 23–30 hours

Diet From small aquatic insects and other invertebrates to fish and small birds

Habitat A wide range of freshwater habitats including lakes, pools, and backwaters; some live in caves or wells

Distribution Widely in Africa, parts of the Middle East, and southern and western Asia; as a food or aquarium fish in other regions—for example, Florida and Hawaii

⊕ *The walking catfish (Clarias batrachus) is the best-known member of its family. It is found from India to Indonesia, but has also been introduced elsewhere.*

Walking Catfish

Clariidae

A fish that can walk on dry land and breathe air? Not a biological impossibility for most of the species of walking catfish, which have developed systems that can exploit conditions both in and out of water.

THE ABILITY OF WALKING CATFISH to survive out of water comes about because the gills, or parts of the gills, are specially modified to enable the fish to breathe not just in normally oxygenated water but also in polluted, oxygen-poor conditions. Provided the air is sufficiently humid to keep the gill chamber moist and prevent the scaleless, mucus-covered body from drying out, walking catfish can even survive for a time out of water. They can certainly live out of water long enough for them to walk from one stretch of water to another, using a combination of their pectoral fin spines and eel-like body movements. Walking catfish can also survive periods of drought buried in the mud at the bottom of dried-out pools until the rains return—which may be for several months or more in the hotter, drier areas of their range.

Air-breathing Equipment

All four gills, but particularly the second and fourth, are modified in walking catfish. As well as the normal gill tissue, all the gills have a flap known as the respiratory membrane extending upward into a chamber (the suprabranchial chamber) located above the gills. They also carry a respiratory "fan" that is especially elaborate on the fourth gill arch, whose normal gill tissue is much reduced. Also, parts of the second and fourth gill arches have developed into a finely branched, treelike structure known as the arborescent organ, which is suspended in the suprabranchial chamber.

So while the gills absorb dissolved oxygen from the water in the normal way, the other structures allow walking catfish to absorb oxygen directly from air gulped by the fish at the water's surface. The capacity to breathe in oxygen directly is a major survival tool for the family. If the water in their habitat is polluted or gets too hot, oxygen levels become depleted. Should this happen, walking catfish can switch systems instantly to breathe oxygen from the air. Indeed, some species have become so reliant on their dual-purpose breathing apparatus, they may drown if prevented from breathing surface air from time to time.

The Tree of Life

A walking catfish's arborescent organ, respiratory fan and membrane, and gills perform roughly the same task that lungs do in air-breathing mammals. They are the interface where gas exchange (carbon dioxide for oxygen) takes place. Blood circulates in the fish's body, gradually picking up carbon dioxide. It reaches the arborescent organ and respiratory fan and membrane where the carbon dioxide is released as bubbles through the fish's gill openings, while oxygen is absorbed. Oxygen-rich blood flows from these organs via the superbranchial chamber into the body, where the whole process starts again.

Walking Threat

Walking catfish are widely cultivated as food fish in Africa and Asia. The most popular species is "the" walking catfish, or Asian

⇩ *The walking catfish (Clarias batrachus), also known as the Asian walking catfish, is popular as a food fish. In its albino form it is also kept as an aquarium fish.*

Tree or Labyrinth?

The structure that allows walking catfish to breathe atmospheric oxygen is called the arborescent organ due to its treelike or dendritic (finely branched) nature. In other fish species that take in air at the water's surface, such as the gouramis and their relatives (family Anabantidae), the air-breathing apparatus consists of highly folded plates and is known as the labyrinth organ.

Confusingly, the terms labyrinth organ and arborescent organ are quite frequently used as if they were the same thing. As a result, the walking catfish are often referred to as the labyrinth catfish. However, since the walking catfish do not really have a labyrinth organ, this name should be dropped. More accurately, walking catfish are also referred to as air-breathing catfish.

⊙ *This African walking catfish, only partially submerged in shallows in South Africa's Kruger National Park, is probably spawning.*

walking catfish (*Clarias batrachus*), which grows to around 22 inches (55 cm) and is a voracious predator. In the U.S. the albino form of the species became quite popular as an aquarium fish, although less so as a food fish. However, sale of the species is now banned throughout the country, along with all other members of its family, being regarded as "injurious to wildlife."

This is due to the fact that the fish may travel from a polluted water source to a clean one, possibly bringing the pollution with them. There is also concern because walking catfish not only survive where other fish and aquatic creatures may not, but can reproduce rapidly. However, moving from one source of water to another is not always linked to pollution or lack of oxygen. Sometimes it may be due to a lack of food, whose composition in the case of many of the walking catfish is wide ranging and can include insects as well as other fish.

Put all these factors together, and it is evident that walking catfish can present a real threat to native species should they escape and become established in the wild. This in fact is what happened in Florida, where fish that escaped or were released in the period between 1965 and 1967 resulted in most freshwater habitats in the southern half of the state being contaminated by the late 1970s.

Closer to its native waters in Asia, the Asian walking catfish is itself under threat from introduced species such as the much larger African walking catfish (*Clarias gareipinus*), a native of the African Nile and Niger Rivers. It is not just the fear that African walking catfish may replace its Asian cousin that is causing concern, but the fact that these two species can interbreed. Should this become widespread, the genetic integrity of Asian walking catfish could be seriously harmed.

On the other hand, controlled hybridization of the African walking catfish and the large-headed walking catfish (*Clarias macrocephalus*) has been achieved so successfully by aquaculturists that the hybrid has become one of the most popular food fish in countries such as Malaysia and Thailand.

Less Famous Walkers

The *Clarias* genus, containing around 45 species, is the best-known group of the clariids. Little known outside scientific circles are the eel-like species, such as the eel catfish (*Channallabes apus*) and the flathead eel catfish (*Gymnallabes typus*). Two other pink, eyeless species that prefer underground waters are *Horaglanis krishnai,* found in wells around Kottayam in Kerala, India, and *Uegitglanis zammaranoi* from Somalia. The most famous cave-dwelling species is the cave catfish (*Clarias cavernicola*).

⬆ *At 4.6 feet (1.4 m) in length and a weight of 132 pounds (60 kg) the African walking catfish (*Clarias gareipinus*) is one of the largest in its family. It has become very popular as a food fish.*

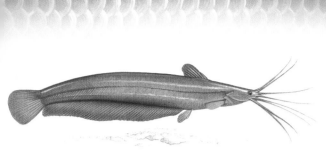

Airsac Catfish

Heteropneustes fossilis

Graceful, elegant, but deceptively dangerous, the whiskered airsac catfish packs enough venom to kill a human being. It also has a bad temper, seeking out victims and attacking without provocation.

Common name Airsac catfish (stinging, liver, or fossil catfish)

Scientific name *Heteropneustes fossilis*

Family Heteropneustidae

Order Siluriformes

Size Up to 12 in (30 cm)

Key features Elongated body; flattened head; 4 pairs of long barbels; short-based dorsal fin; pectoral fins with venomous spines; adipose fin missing or present as a low ridge; internally the fish possesses an elongated airsac extending back into the body from the gill chamber

Breeding Eggs laid in a depression prepared in shallow water by both parents; eggs and young defended by both adults; eggs take about 2 days to hatch; offspring guarded up to 1 month

Diet Wide-ranging—small fish, insects, and aquatic invertebrates

Habitat Mainly in slow-flowing or still waters, swamps, rice paddies, and ditches; often in turbid water

Distribution Widely in Bangladesh, India, Pakistan, Laos, Myanmar, Sri Lanka, Thailand, and possibly Nepal

SOME ANIMALS (INCLUDING SOME FISH) are described as passive stingers—in other words, they only sting if attacked or handled. However, the airsac catfish has the reputation of being an active stinger and is reported to be pugnacious and aggressive, almost as if it was "spoiling for a fight." Although it seems likely that the reputation may be exaggerated, there are reports from rice-paddy workers who claim that the catfish attacks without provocation. There is probably some truth here; but however active or otherwise the airsac catfish is in terms of attacks, there is no doubt that its sting is at best extremely painful and, at worst, can actually result in the death of the victim.

Defending Yourself

The damage is caused by venom being injected into a wound inflicted by the powerful pectoral fin spines. Due care must therefore be taken when handling the fish. Most of the people who live in close proximity to airsac catfish are

⊕ The airsac catfish is also known as the liver catfish because of its liver-brown coloration, making it hard to see in muddy streams and ditches.

probably well aware of the dangers and take appropriate precautions when they can. For example, in India, where large numbers of the fish are used for human consumption, food preparers avoid being stung because they know what parts of the fish to avoid or remove when cooking it.

However, it is quite a different matter in the turbid waters of the fish's home, where there is a real risk of accidentally stepping on an airsac catfish, particularly during the breeding season. At such times the catfish guard their nests, eggs, and young, and will therefore attack any intruder.

Exclusive Family

The heteropneustids form the smallest of all the catfish families. This is especially true if there is only one species, rather than the two usually quoted. The airsac catfish is a species with wide Asian distribution that has been known to science since 1794. However, some 70 years later a much smaller airsac catfish from Sri Lankan waters was described and labeled *Heteropneustes microps*. It was very similar to the original airsac catfish but around half its size. It is now known from just a few sites around Dambuwa, close to the western coast of the southern half of the island. It was found sharing pools with the airsac catfish, accounting for just 2 percent of the total *Heteropneustes*

population. The only features that distinguished *H.microps* from its larger relative were its smaller size and the fact that its anal and caudal fins were joined.

However, studies carried out during the 1990s found that if a sample of specimens from a normal catch of airsac catfish was examined, around 2 percent of them also had the anal and caudal fins joined up. When the fish were analyzed in detail, it was found that they had all suffered an injury that caused the two fins to regrow joined together rather than separate. Scientists concluded therefore that the two species were one and the same; *H. microps* was simply an example of *H. fossilis* that had been injured during its early growth.

Hot Water Remedy

Some fish poisons, while still causing excruciating pain, can have their effects neutralized by high temperatures. This does not necessarily eliminate all the consequences of a sting, but it can be an effective method of first aid, providing victims with some precious time during which they can seek professional help.

Hot temperatures denature the venom. Therefore the usual advice consists of placing the affected part of the body in water that is as hot as the victim can bear. This will rapidly neutralize the poison in the immediate area of the wound, thus reducing the overall dose of venom. However, hot water has no effect on venom that is already circulating around the body via the bloodstream. Hot baths are therefore only one of the measures that need to be taken; prompt medical attention is also needed.

Frogmouth Catfish

Chacidae

A frogmouth catfish may not be beautiful and may spend much of its life motionless on the bottom, but it has two secrets: in-built fishing bait and jet propulsion.

Indian frogmouth catfish (*Chaca chaca*)

Common name Frogmouth catfish (angler catfish, squarehead catfish)

Family Chacidae

Order Siluriformes

Number of species 3 in 1 genus

Size Around 8 in (20 cm); some may grow larger

Key features Flattened head; large, straight-edged, upward-pointing mouth; 3 or 4 pairs of barbels; very small eyes located on top of head; dorsal fin possesses stout, short serrated spine; pectoral fins possess a similar spine; adipose fin joined with caudal fin; body coloration mottled dark brown or blackish

Breeding No details available

Diet Almost exclusively fish

Habitat Slow-flowing or still waters with soft substrate; frequently mud

Distribution Bangladesh, Borneo, India, Indonesia, Malaysia, Myanmar, and Nepal

⊕ *The Indian frogmouth catfish (Chaca chaca), sometimes described as resembling a flattened leaf with a huge mouth at one end. Its tiny eyes help it avoid being spotted.*

ALTHOUGH THEY USE DIFFERENT "FISHING TACKLE," frogmouth catfish are just as successful at catching prey as the sea-based anglerfish (order Lophiiformes). Instead of the angler fish's "rod," frogmouth catfish wiggle their short maxillary barbels in a jerky movement to simulate worms. So effective is this technique that victims fall for it in sufficient numbers to maintain healthy populations of the three species that make up this specialized family of catfish.

Making the hunting technique even more efficient is an upturned mouth whose size must be seen to be believed. It is so large that it appears capable of taking in prey almost the same size as the frogmouth catfish itself.

Jet-propelled Cats

Frogmouth catfish also have another use for their huge, gaping mouths. Like most of their relatives, they normally use their caudal fin to propel themselves over short distances. However, situations often arise when an extra burst of speed or an injection of more power may be needed: for example, being confronted by a thick mass of vegetation or fleeing from a predator. At such times frogmouth catfish turn their large mouths and small gill openings into an efficient jet-propulsion device.

To use the technique, the fish first takes large gulps of water into its mouth, then clamps it shut, generating a sudden buildup of pressure that needs an escape route. The escape route is provided by the gill openings. However, because the gill openings are small, they cannot release all the water at once. Instead, it is forced out in a narrow, powerful stream, propelling the fish forward in a lightning-fast burst of speed. The jet is strong enough to get the fish through an

↗ *An Indian frogmouth catfish (Chaca chaca) displaying its huge mouth. Normally sedentary, frogmouth catfish can move with surprising speed and power when necessary.*

 SEE ALSO Anglerfish **36**:74; Catfish, Banjo **37**:92

obstruction or whisk it out of the path of a predator.

Although they are unusual in having jet-propulsive qualities, frogmouths are not unique in this respect. The banjo catfish (family Aspredinidae) have also perfected a similar technique, but probably not to the same degree as the chacids.

Frogmouth, Squarehead, or Angler Catfish?

The members of the family Chacidae have at least three common names. First there is frogmouth catfish, a name which has more to do with the fact that one species, the Indian frogmouth catfish, makes a croaking sound when it is removed from the water. Strictly speaking, the sound is more of a "chaca chaca chaca" (hence the scientific name) than a croak. The mouth, although wide and cavernous, is straight-edged and therefore quite different from that possessed by most frogs.

Second, the name angler catfish refers to the ability of the species to lure prey using their barbels as bait. Last, squarehead catfish is undoubtedly the most accurate name, since it best describes the shape of the head in all three species. The other two species in the family are the Malaysian or chocolate frogmouth catfish (*Chaca bankanensis*) and the Burmese frogmouth catfish (*C. burmensis*).

Other Defenses

In addition to their jet-propelled tactics, frogmouth catfish use two other forms of defense. The first one, which is perfectly adequate in most situations, involves doing absolutely nothing at all. The dull body coloring and flattened body shape blend in so well with the surroundings that a frogmouth will usually remain totally motionless on the bottom, as invisible to a potential attacker as it is to its prey. Frogmouths rely so heavily on this concealment technique that they will often refuse to move even when prodded.

If the concealment strategy fails, and if it is impossible to make a swift jet-propelled escape, the second, rather riskier form of defense comes into play. The frogmouth lets itself be taken into its predator's mouth. Once inside, the frogmouth raises its powerful, short, serrated (saw-edged) dorsal fin spine, presenting its attacker with a painful, awkward mouthful that is soon spat out.

Electric catfish (*Malapterurus electricus*)

Common name Electric catfish

Family Malapteruridae

Order Siluriformes

Number of species 11 in 1 genus

Size From around 4.8 in (12.2 cm) to around 48 in (1.2 m)

Key features Sturdy head; small eyes; fleshy lips; 3 pairs of mouth barbels; nasal or "nose" barbels lacking; no dorsal fin; adipose fin well formed and located near the tail; rounded caudal fin; different degrees and intensity of mottling and body banding

Breeding May spawn in burrows excavated in river banks

Diet Smaller fish

Habitat Slow-moving or still waters containing rocks, sunken logs, and roots where the fish can shelter or rest in daylight hours; many preferred waters are tannin-stained (known as blackwaters) or turbid in nature

Distribution Widespread in tropical Africa from western Africa through central regions to the Nile River; individual species may have restricted ranges

⊕ *The electric catfish* (Malapterurus electricus), *a fierce 4-ft (1.2-m) predator widespread in tropical Africa. The electricity it produces is not only used to stun prey and deter predators but also to navigate and detect prey.*

CATFISH

Electric Catfish — Malapteruridae

Often described as large sausages that lie on the bottom doing very little, the electric catfish will knock you back as no sausage can—as unsuspecting humans have frequently found to their cost.

ELECTRICITY GENERATION IS NOT UNIQUE to electric catfish. Numerous fish in many unrelated families employ electricity for various purposes. Many, like the elephantnoses (family Mormyridae), generate weak electrical fields to help them navigate and communicate. At the other end of the electric spectrum the electric eel can produce around 550 volts.

Somewhere in between the weak and the most powerful generators lies the electric catfish, capable of producing bursts of around 350 volts. Such a level of electricity, while not strong enough to kill, is nevertheless powerful enough to stun prey, deter predators, or leave a human hurt or temporarily shocked.

Organic Generator

In electric catfish the organ that generates electricity lies under the skin and occupies an area (on both sides of the body) extending from behind the head to a point approximately in line with the front edges of the adipose and anal fins, ending in a backward-pointing arc. It does not, however, extend into the fins. The organ consists of specialized cells called electrocytes that have evolved from pectoral (chest) muscle cells. The electrocytes are about 0.4 inches (1 cm) in diameter and are stacked on top of each other. One surface of each electrocyte carries a short stalk and is attached to fine nerve fibers. Each stack of cells is enveloped in a jellylike substance and receives a rich blood supply. Each complete organ is, in turn, attached to a large nerve end that arises from the front part of the spinal cord. Because of their orientation and the front attachment of the main nerves the current in the electric catfish's organ flows from front to back.

⊖ *An electric catfish (Malapterurus electricus) from Lake Tanganyika, Tanzania. In its mouth is its stunned prey.*

⊕ *Smallmouth electric catfish (Malapterurus microstoma) from the northern region of the Zambezi River. Electric catfish hide by day, but at dusk they start to spread out and search for food.*

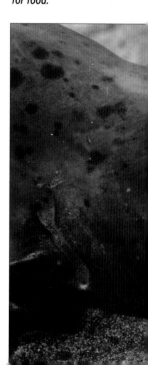

SEE ALSO Elephantnoses and Whales **31**:106; Knifefish, Electric **33**:98; Catfish, Bagrid **37**:22

In addition to the electric organ's function in stunning prey and deterring predators, it also has other functions. It can, for instance, be used in navigation and detecting prey—two activities that do not require the strong pulses that defense and attack demand. In addition, electric catfish use the versatile organ to size up rivals, intruders, and potential mates. However, in the case of a potential adversary it is only employed if other, more moderate, and nonelectrical measures have failed to supply the information or deter the rival.

The longest-lasting discharges the electric organ can generate are the ones used for stunning or hunting; they can last up to 30 seconds and consist of several hundred individual pulses. The pulses are sometimes preceded by a series of weaker ones that the electric catfish may send out to help flush prey into the open.

The Father of Thunder

The properties of the electric catfish were well known to ancient Africans. In fact, the Arabic name for the electric catfish translates as "Father of Thunder." It is also recorded in Egyptian hieroglyphics some 5,000 years old, in which its name translates as "He who had saved many in the sea." It is not clear why the fish was referred to in such terms, although it is known that it was—and still is—used to treat a variety of medical conditions. Reportedly, electric catfish can be placed on the affected part of the body to effect a cure. Quite how this treatment is intended to work is something of a mystery, especially in cases in which live shock-producing fish are used.

Electric Catfish Species

Common Name	Scientific Name	Approx. Size inches (cm)
	M. beninensis	8.8 (22.3)
	M. cavalliensis	4.8 (12.2)
Electric catfish	M. electricus	48 (122.0)
	M. leonensis	6.1 (15.5)
Smallmouth electric catfish	M. microstoma	27.2 (69.0)
	M. minjiriya	40.2 (102.0)
	M. monsembeensis	22.8 (58.0)
	M. oguensis	6.3 (16.1)
	M. shirensis	12 (30.0)
	M. tanganyikaensis	19.1 (48.5)
	M. tanoensis	10.2 (26.0)

All lengths are standard, in other words, measured from snout to base of caudal fin. However, the figure for the smallmouth electric catfish is for the total length—from snout to tip of caudal fin.

How Many Species?

The first electric catfish to be officially described was *Malapterurus electricus,* in 1789. Since it was believed to be the only species in the genus, it became known, quite simply, as the electric catfish. Three other species were subsequently described during the next 90 years, but they all came to be regarded as varieties of the original electric catfish rather than as separate species. The situation remained like this until 1969, when a new species from Central Africa, the smallmouth electric catfish (*M. microstoma*), was described. It was followed in 1987 by the discovery of yet another species, *M. minjiriya,* from West Africa.

It had long been known that electric catfish were not only widespread in Africa, but that they occurred with variable body markings and sizes. However, the differences had not been examined in detail until 2000. When the study was eventually carried out, it was discovered that the electric catfish group consisted of not one, two, or even three species but 11 (see box "Electric Catfish Species"). The main differences between the species are in the overall body length and patterning, the shape and size of the mouth, the tooth arrangement, and the number of vertebrae in the skeleton.

Changing Data

The results of the investigations have opened a whole new chapter in electric catfish history, raising the need for further in-depth studies of each of the new species, especially since some are restricted in their distribution. It has also, of course, changed the distribution map for the electric catfish itself. This species is still the most widespread of all, but many populations of electric catfish once believed to be isolated pockets of *M. electricus* now turn out to be populations of other species. For example, the electric catfish from the Ogôoué basin in Gabon are now known to be the only representatives of the species *M. oguensis*. Similarly, those from the Cavally River on the Ivory Coast are members of the species *M. cavalliensis*, and at least some of the individuals from the Zambezi River basin belong to the species *M. shirensis*.

Little-known Properties

In contrast to the considerable data available on the electrical qualities of electric catfish, disappointingly little is known about other aspects of their biology and affinities.

They are, for example, believed to share some characteristics with the bagrid catfish (family Bagridae), the shark catfish (family Pangasiidae), and the sheatfish (family Siluridae). In fact, the original scientific name for *Malapterurus electricus* was *Silurus electricus*. More research is required on the possible links, however, so the best we can say is that the closest relatives of the electric catfish probably belong to one of the above families.

Of one thing there can be no doubt: Electric catfish are highly aggressive toward each other. They are also keenly predatory, using their electrical equipment to catch prey that they would otherwise be unable to catch largely owing to their lack of speed.

The electric catfish was first imported from Africa into Europe in 1904. It has enjoyed a long history as an aquarium fish, but it has proved impossible to breed the species, or any of its close relatives, in captivity. Details about its breeding season and habits in the wild are also very scarce. It is variously reported to breed during the summer season or during the rainy season. Perhaps both are correct and apply either to the electric catfish in different parts of its distribution or to one or other of the new species that had previously been thought to be variants of the electric catfish.

Intriguing Stories

Breeding is thought to take place in excavated cavities or inside holes in river banks. The holes or burrows measure up to 10 feet (3 m) in length and occur in water ranging between 40 inches (1 m) and 10 feet (3 m) in depth. The electric catfish is reported to form pairs prior to spawning, but no details are available for the other species. However, owing to the former misidentification of species, it is possible that the scant data we have for the electric catfish may also apply to the ten other members of the genus. Intriguingly, one report suggests that the electric catfish may be a mouthbrooder, but this is also unconfirmed.

⊕ *An electric catfish (Malapterurus electricus) showing the color variation and striping sometimes seen in the genus.*

Hardhead sea catfish (*Ariopsis felis*)

Common name	Sea catfish (salmon catfish, shark catfish, fork-tailed catfish, crucifix fish)
Family	Ariidae
Order	Siluriformes
Number of species	120–150 in around 14 genera
Size	From around 9.8 in (25 cm) to around 4.3 ft (1.8 m)
Key features	Elongated with scaleless body; head usually depressed, flattened, or conically shaped with bony shield; 2 or 3 pairs of barbels present; dorsal and pectoral fins possess stout serrated spines that cause painful wounds; adipose fin present; caudal fin well forked
Breeding	In mouthbrooding species females develop modifications on anal fin during breeding season; eggs often "marble-sized"; incubated orally by male for 4 weeks or longer
Diet	Predatory, wide selection of prey animals and fish
Habitat	Estuaries, coastal lagoons, and in coastal waters; some exclusively freshwater; many move between habitats; habitats contain sandy or muddy bottoms
Distribution	Extremely wide in tropical and subtropical waters; may be found in temperate zones during summer

⤒ *The hardhead sea catfish (Ariopsis felis), a streamlined fish that lives along the west Atlantic coast. It feeds at night on crabs, shrimp, and small fish.*

CATFISH

Sea Catfish

Ariidae

In some South American countries small, elaborately decorated bone objects depicting a crucifix are sold. The bones come from sea catfish which, among other names, are also known as crucifix fish.

MEMBERS OF THE FAMILY ARIIDAE tend to be active swimmers always on the move. Many of the species are found in fresh water, while others occur in estuaries and even in true marine conditions. They usually swim gracefully, with their dorsal fin fully erect.

The habits and appearance of ariids, plus the large sizes that some species can attain, are the reasoning behind four of the common names for the family. The first name, sea catfish, came about because the Ariidae is one of two families of catfish containing truly marine species.

The second name, salmon catfish, comes from the observation that salmon spend some of their lives in the sea and some in fresh water, and so do some ariids. The grayish color of many species, the erect dorsal fin, constant motion, elegant swimming movements, and large size all help explain the third name, shark catfish. The name fork-tailed catfish refers to the distinct and relatively large caudal fin possessed by all ariids.

Difficult IDs

Within the family the largest genus by far is *Arius*. However, it is also perhaps the most difficult to identify with absolute accuracy. Despite general shared characteristics, some *Arius* species may have two rather than three pairs of barbels. Some have a furrow or groove covered by a flap of skin across the snout, and others do not. Some may have small, pointed teeth on the palate (roof of the mouth), and others may have more molar-shaped teeth on the palate. Some have no teeth at all. Because of the differences, some experts have attempted to split *Arius* species into several

⤓ *The erect, sharklike dorsal fin of a sea catfish shows how the family acquired one of its common names.*

separate genera. Such variation is not surprising when it is considered that *Arius* is so widely distributed. One species, *A. jatius*, is known to occur in the Ganges, while the shark catfish (*A. seemanni*) is found in river estuaries in the northern regions of South America; another species, *A. sciurus*, has been found in the Tapi River in Thailand, while *A. truncatus* is known from Java; *A. fuscus* occurs on the island of Madagascar, *A. maculatus* comes from Japan, and *A. graeffei*—the blue catfish—is from northern Australia. And they are only a few examples taken from the 150 or so species that are regarded by some authorities as belonging to the genus *Arius*.

Mysterious Mouthbrooders

Sea catfish are remarkable breeders. For a start, they produce huge eggs measuring almost 0.6 inches (1.4 cm) in diameter. They are supplied with rich yolk that sustains the developing embryos until they hatch. It is not known exactly how long eggs take to hatch because after laying, the males actually take up the fertilized eggs, which could number well over 100, into their mouths and brood them there for around four weeks. At this stage newly born young can be observed, some measuring nearly 1 inch (2.5 cm) in length and still attached to their dwindling yolk supply.

Even at this early stage, though, the young possess well-developed barbels. The male will then continue brooding and generally caring for the young for another two weeks or so, the duration depending on the species.

Unanswered Questions

Although we have details like the above at our disposal, many questions regarding the breeding behavior of ariids remain unanswered and await further studies. For example, what role is played by the anal fin modifications that females develop during the breeding season? They include a thickened flap and red coloration—features that both apparently disappear after a successful mating. Furthermore, how do the eggs get from the female's genital opening into the male's mouth? And when and how are the eggs fertilized? Does the female hold the eggs within the flap while the male fertilizes them? Does the female produce her large eggs singly or in batches?

Chosen Fish

The "crucifix" part of another of the ariids' common names derives from the large bone in the skull, the parasphenoid. The bone is more or less cross-shaped in most fish, but it is particularly so in some ariid catfish. Crucifix fish skulls are highly prized by many people.

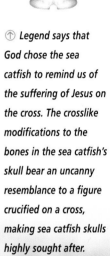

⬆ *Legend says that God chose the sea catfish to remind us of the suffering of Jesus on the cross. The crosslike modifications to the bones in the sea catfish's skull bear an uncanny resemblance to a figure crucified on a cross, making sea catfish skulls highly sought after.*

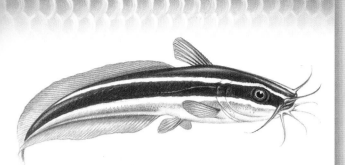

Coral catfish (*Plotosus lineatus*)

Tandan Catfish   Plotosidae

Beware of buzzing coral; it has not been colonized by a swarm of bees but a shoal of coral catfish (Plotosus lineatus). The "aquatic bees" sting with such severity that it can take months for the wound to heal.

Common name Tandan catfish (eeltail catfish, coral catfish, stinging catfish)

Family Plotosidae

Order Siluriformes

Number of species Around 32 in 9 genera

Size From around 4.8 in (12.2 cm) to about 35.4 in (90 cm)

Key features Elongate body, almost eel-like in some genera; flattened or rounded head; 4 pairs of barbels; dorsal and pectoral fins bear a serrated, venomous spine at the front; adipose fin absent; anal and caudal fin joined; top part of caudal fin extends forward along back as a caudodorsal fin with soft rays

Breeding Little known generally; dewfish (*Tandanus tandanus*) well known

Diet Animal matter, including insects, snails, crustaceans, fish, and other invertebrates

Habitat Wide range, from coral reefs through estuaries to rivers; around 50 percent of species strictly freshwater

Distribution Indian Ocean and western Pacific Ocean extending from Japan to Australia

A WELL-DOCUMENTED ACCOUNT OF SOMEONE being stung by a tandan catfish occurred in 1949. A biologist named A. Herre was stung by a catfish less than 6 inches (15 cm) long that had been lying in the bottom of his boat for about 15 minutes. Assuming the fish was dead, Herre picked it up. Thereupon the fish struggled and stung him on the thumb with one of its pectoral fin spines.

The pain, although considerable, did not prevent Herre from fishing for another half hour or so. However, during this time the pain got worse, as did the swelling—not just of the thumb but eventually the whole hand, wrist, and forearm. The problem became so serious that the swelling had to be medically drained, and Herre was

⊕ *The coral catfish (Plotosus lineatus) grows to about 12 inches (30 cm) and lives at the bottom of reefs and estuaries. In spite of its venomous spines, it is a popular aquarium fish.*

These black tandan (*Neosilurus ater*), found in the seas off north Australia, perfectly display the "megafin," in which the caudal and anal fins are joined. The fused fin is a typical identifying feature of tandan catfish.

given a potent morphine painkiller. It took nearly a week for the swelling to go down. Other complications included three days of severe diarrhea and weight loss. After this critical week-long phase almost six months passed before a full recovery was made.

The species responsible for giving Herre such a hard time is the saltwater or coral catfish (*Plotosus lineatus*). It is a particularly beautiful species during its juvenile stages, when it is strikingly marked in dark brown and cream-colored stripes running from head to tail. The stripes disappear with age, and the fish become uniformly dark.

Joined Tandans

Not all members of the family are sea going; nor are they all as dangerous as the coral catfish. In fact, the genus *Tandanus*, which contains about 12 species, inhabits a range of habitats, from fully marine through estuarine to fresh water. The most typical species, the dewfish (*Tandanus tandanus*), is, like the majority of its relatives, strictly a freshwater species. Unlike the coral catfish, it is not easily alarmed and is therefore less of a threat, although its venom is probably just as potent.

Like all the tandan catfish, the dewfish has joined caudal and anal fins. Although there is

→ *The toothless catfish (Anodontiglanis dahli) is a native of northern Australian rivers. The pointed head and almost eel-like body give rise to yet another description of fish in the family: eeltail catfish. The dorsal fin has serrated, venomous spines that protect the catfish from predators.*

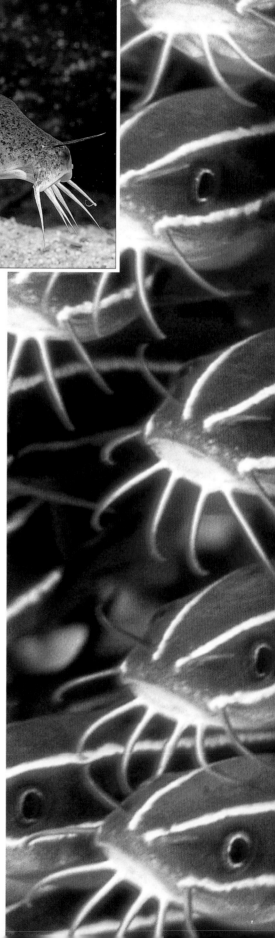

no adipose fin, the top front end of the caudal fin extends some way forward along the back of the body. This extension is regarded as a second dorsal fin (it contains rays and is therefore quite unlike an adipose fin) and is often referred to as the caudodorsal fin. The joined "megafin," allied to the elongated body form and the four pairs of well-formed mouth barbels, have given rise to yet another name for the Plotosidae: the eeltail catfish.

→ *Juvenile coral catfish (Plotosus lineatus) bunch together in a ball for protection while they are still small and vulnerable, and their stinging abilities have not fully developed.*

Dewfish Breeders

The dewfish is the one of the few members of the family in which breeding behavior is understood. The male excavates large, circular nests, some measuring up to 40 inches (1 m) in spring and summer, usually in the sandy or muddy substrata of freshwater estuaries or rivers. There may be large numbers of small rocks and coarse gravel around the edge of the nests, and the insides may also be filled with gravel, stones, and vegetation. A male will seek out a female and chase or drive her to the completed nest. Upward of 20,000 eggs may be laid by a single medium-sized female. After laying, the male takes up nest-guarding duty. Hatching takes about one week, but the male may guard the site for up to 18 days.

In the coral catfish, a marine species, eggs may be laid during summer, either in a nest or in rock crevices. Either way, the nest and the eggs are protected by the male, and hatching takes 7 to 10 days.

"Bumblebee" Balls

Juvenile coral catfish regularly come together to form tight balls, sometimes consisting of hundreds of specimens, with each fish's head pointing toward the center. The balls are capable of moving in one direction or another as if they were a single organism, earning themselves the nickname of "catfish going to church," an imaginative tag coined by Australian Aboriginal children.

Another name used for the colorful, ball-making juveniles is the bumblebee catfish because of their color (although the light stripes are not yellow, as in bumblebees, and the stripes run from head to tail rather than vertically), their swimming behavior, and their ability to make buzzing sounds as they swim through the coral reefs.

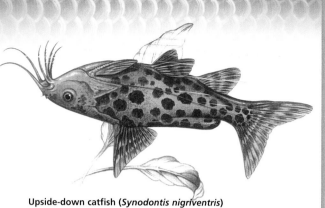

Upside-down catfish (*Synodontis nigriventris*)

Common name Upside-down catfish (squeakers, squeaking
catfish)

Family Mochokidae

Order Siluriformes

Number of species Around 170 in 10 genera

Size From around 2 in (5 cm) to around 27.5 in
(70 cm)

Key features Normal-headed species have sloping forehead
and slightly to moderately pointed snout; mouth
on underside of tip of snout; in sucker-mouthed
species mouth is broader and more straight-
edged with fleshy lips and broad tooth pads;
stout cephalic (head) shield found in all,
extending to front of dorsal fin along the top
and to the base of pectoral fins along the sides
and bottom; 3 pairs of barbels (no nasal barbels),
ornate in some; dorsal and pectoral fins possess
a stout spine at front, can be "locked" in
defense; adipose fin large, becoming sail like in
normal-headed species

Breeding Few details available; eggs said to be adhesive
and laid under cover; no parental care reported;
hatching takes about a week; at least 2 species
lay eggs among those laid by breeding
mouthbrooding cichlids

Diet Small organisms, crustaceans, and plankton;
algae scraped off rocks, logs, and submerged
vegetation; larger species take small fish

Habitat Prefer slow-moving waters, lakes, and swamps;
sucker-mouthed species prefer faster-flowing
waters, some in torrents; many spend day hiding
under submerged logs and roots or in caves and
crevices

Distribution Widespread in most tropical regions of Africa
including African Rift lakes

⬆ *The 4-inch (10-cm) upside-down catfish (Synodontis
nigriventris) swims upside down to graze the underside of
leaves for algae and tiny animals.*

CATFISH

Upside-down Catfish

Mochokidae

*Some mochokids have the habit of flipping onto
their backs and swimming around upside down
as if they are sick or injured.*

UNUSUAL THOUGH IT APPEARS, SWIMMING in an
inverted fashion is natural behavior for upside-
down catfish. They do not do it all the time,
however; even the most famous species of
upside-down catfish, *Synodontis nigriventris*,
does not spend its whole life inverted, but it
does swim in this way more frequently than
do any other species in the family.

In fact, the habit is such an integral and
frequent part of the lifestyle of *S. nigriventris*
that the fish has developed reverse countershading (see box "Now You See Me...Now You
Don't"). Instead of the normal body shading
pattern consisting of a dark back and a lighter
belly, this species, whose species name
nigriventris means "black belly," exhibits the
opposite arrangement—a dark underside and
a lighter back.

The upside-down swimming habit of the
family, and probably that of others which adopt
a similar swimming orientation, is not present at
birth and may take a few months to develop.

Normal Heads and Suckers

Although the name upside-down catfish is
certainly descriptive of some species and has
made mochokids famous the world over, the
behavior is not exhibited by the majority of
members. Indeed, it is possible that more
species are capable of squeaking than flipping
over, making the alternative name for the
family—squeakers or squeaking catfish—
probably more accurate if less colorful.

Two distinct groups are identified within
the family Mochokidae. The first group contains
species that have what are described as
"normal" heads. The other group consists of

⬇ *Swimming close to
the bottom, a beautifully
marked polkadot
squeaker (Synodontis
angelicus) shows the
sloping forehead and
ornate barbels typical of
the "normal-headed"
species.*

the suckermouthed species; they have flattened heads and, as their common name indicates, sucker-type mouths.

The normal-headed group is the larger of the two, and it contains seven genera: *Acanthocleithron*, *Brachysynodontis*, *Hemisynodontis*, *Microsynodontis*, *Mochokiella*, *Mochokus,* and *Synodontis*—the last genus being by far the largest, with 70 percent of all the species in the family. It is the genus to which the upside-down catfish *S. nigriventris* and its closest relatives belong. The normal-headed group includes the smallest of the squeakers—Payne's synodontis or the African bumblebee catfish (*Mochokiella paynei*), which grows to a maximum size of 2 inches (5 cm),

Now You See Me...Now You Don't

A fish that is uniformly drab will immediately stand out. In normal sunlight the back of the fish contrasts against the darkness of the water below it, making it visible to predators from above, such as seabirds. The lower half of the body, in shade, will also be darker than the bright background created by the sunlight from above, making the fish visible to predators, such as larger fish, approaching from below. Viewed from the side, the light top and darker lower half created by the sunlight striking the uniformly colored body makes it visible to predators at any angle. One of the most common ways that has evolved allowing species to avoid the attentions of predators is the development of a body patterning that helps them become less visible. In fish, reducing visibility by body patterning is achieved in three ways. Some fish have an almost totally transparent body. Others have a reflective body—in other words, one with silvery scales on the flanks. The other method is to adopt countershading on the body: having darker colors on the back fading to light colors along the belly. The effectiveness of each of the methods, or even a combination of them, depends on a number of factors, including the habits of the fish, its surroundings, and the intensity of ambient light.

The majority of fish species exhibit countershading to great effect. The darker colors along the back absorb light waves from above and make the fish appear virtually invisible against the equally dark background of the water or bottom below. Viewed at any angle, ranging from directly above through horizontal to varying angles from below, the dark-to-light body shading provides effective camouflage against the changing levels of light intensity that exist (in reverse) at these orientations. Similarly, from directly below white or light belly colors make the fish hard to see as it blends into the bright background created by light filtering through the sky.

Countershading is a proven, effective survival mechanism. But some fish—such as the upside-down catfish and their relatives—have the opposite color arrangement. In other words, they have dark bellies and lighter colored backs, which would normally make them stand out from every angle. But such fish are designed to swim upside down; and when they do so, the reverse countershading provides the same level of concealment that it affords species that swim in the more "conventional" manner.

⊕ *Upside-down catfish (Synodontis nigriventris) give a spontaneous display of their unusual swimming skills, which from birth take up to eight weeks to develop. This allows them to exploit a food niche other species ignore— algae and other aquatic microorganisms found on the underside of aquatic plants.*

but is usually smaller. It also contains some of the largest, such as the gray synodontis (*Synodontis schall*), which attains 22 inches (56 cm) or more in length, and the black-spotted dusky synodontis (*S. acanthomias)* at around 24 inches (60 cm) in length.

In the normal-headed genera the mouth is located just under the tip of the snout and is surrounded by three pairs of barbels (the nasal or "nose" pair is lacking). In some species the barbels may be quite elaborate: Some bear membranes or flaps, and others are feathery. The head is also protected with a hard body

shield that generally extends to the front of the dorsal fin at the top and to the pectoral fins below. This characteristic arrangement is found in both of the mochokid groups.

In the suckermouth species the barbels tend to be short and much simpler in form. Suckermouths also have characteristic broad, flattened mouths with spread-out lips and pads of scraping teeth. Such an arrangement allows them to cling securely to rocks while they are busy scraping food from them. There are only three genera of suckermouth squeakers: *Atopochilus,* which contains seven or so species; *Chiloglanis,* the 34 or so catlets; and *Euchilichthys,* which contains the three false chiloglanis species.

Like normal-headed mochokids, all the suckermouths have well-formed adipose fins. However, the level of development is nowhere near as sophisticated as that shown by their cousins, which exhibit truly magnificent, almost sail-like adipose fins.

Cuckoo Breeders

A most unusual birdlike breeding strategy has evolved in at least two species of *Synodontis,* the even-spotted synodontis (*S.petricola*), which grows to 22 inches (56 cm) or more, and the cuckoo synodontis (*S. multipunctatus*). Both are whitish fish liberally spotted with black, and both occur in Lake Tanganyika in Africa.

The lake is famous for its spectacular mouthbrooding cichlids. In the breeding season the cichlids go through an elaborate courtship ritual that is routinely exploited by the two enterprising catfish species. After mating, the female cichlid takes the eggs into her mouth and incubates them there until they hatch. Following the hatching and release of the fry, the mother will continue taking her young into her mouth for several more days, or even weeks, whenever danger threatens, thus providing them with an exceptionally high level of protection .

The even-spotted synodontis and the cuckoo synodontis synchronize their breeding with that of several of the mouthbrooding cichlids, following them around as they prepare for spawning. Once spawning gets under way, mouthbrooding cichlids become so focused on the job in hand that they tend to ignore almost anything going on around them, and this is precisely what the parasitic catfish have been waiting for.

As soon as some cichlid eggs have been laid, the catfish dive in between the mating cichlids and release some eggs of their own. It is reported that the catfish eat or steal some of the cichlid eggs before laying their own. Whether this happens or not, the female cichlid picks up any eggs that she sees and incubates

them in her mouth whether they are her own or those laid by the *Synodontis* species. It is estimated that *Synodontis* eggs account for as much as 15 percent of the total brood in one population of the mouth-brooding cichlid *Ctenochromis horei*, one of several mouthbrooding cichlid species to be parasitized by the catfish. The developing *Synodontis* eggs

and fry receive the same level of protection as their cichlid broodmates. It has been suggested that newly hatched synodonts may feed on some of the cichlid eggs or fry. If this turns out to be accurate, the benefits of this parasitic breeding strategy are even higher for the catfish. The parallels with the breeding strategy of the feathered cuckoo are clear.

⬇ *Like the bird for which it is named, the cuckoo synodontis (Synodontis multipunctatus) tricks other species into raising and feeding its young.*

Dolphin catfish (*Pseudodoras niger*)

Common name Talking catfish (thorny catfish)

Family Doradidae

Order Siluriformes

Number of species Around 80–100 in around 35 genera

Size From around 0.5 in (1.3 cm) to around 4 ft (1.2 m)

Key features Robust body; head largely covered by a cephalic shield consisting of several bony plates; species divided into 2 groups depending on head shape; body with a row of hard thorny plates (scutes); most plates contain small, strong backward-pointing "thorns"; dorsal and pectoral fins have prominent, serrated (saw-edged) spine

Breeding Very little known; most details relate to *Amblydoras hancocki*

Diet Many doradids filter bottom sediments, feeding on small invertebrates and plant material; larger species feed on aquatic snails

Habitat Often found over soft substrata into which they can burrow; wide range of waters, including large rivers and flooded forests

Distribution Central and South America—primarily Brazil, Peru, and the Guianas

⬆ *The dolphin catfish (Pseudodoras niger), a narrow-headed doradid, grows to 4 feet (1.2 m) but is a placid creature and eats tiny food particles.*

Talking Catfish
Doradidae

Doradids bristle with defense mechanisms such as saw-edged extensions on the gill covers and bony plate body armor with backward-pointing spines. Even more interesting is the fact that they can "talk."

THE "LANGUAGE" A TALKING CATFISH speaks may not consist of words as we know them, but they certainly express the way the catfish feels. When taken out of the water, talking catfish generally continue opening and shutting their mouths in an exaggerated manner while, at the same time, producing croaking sounds. The behavior can make it appear as though they are actually producing sounds through their mouths. However, the sound comes not from the mouth but either from the pectoral fin spines being moved within their sockets or through the body wall when the swim bladder

⬇ *The most talkative species is Hancock's talking catfish, or Hancock's doradid (Amblydoras hancocki), found chiefly in Peru and Bolivia. It grows to 6 inches (15 cm) in length.*

is vibrated. Depending on the species, talking catfish are capable of producing a range of sounds that have been described as croaking, purring, or chattering.

Problematic Jaguar and Friends

There are between 80 to 100 species in the family Doradidae. The exact number is not known with absolute certainty because there is considerable doubt about the true identity of some species and genera. For instance, the jaguar catfish (*Liosomadoras oncinus*) is very difficult to place, especially since it lacks the thorny body plates that are characteristic of the family Doradidae

In many ways the fish looks like a driftwood catfish (family Auchenipteridae), but it has a larger adipose fin than is typical of the driftwood catfish. In fact, some authorities believe it to lie somewhere in between the two families, while others have argued that the jaguar catfish presents a strong case for joining

the two families and regarding them as one.

Much work remains to be done on the classification of talking catfish. The likely result is that in the end, there will be fewer genera and species within the family.

Dolphin Catfish

One of the largest species in the family is the dolphin catfish (*Pseudodoras niger*): It reportedly reaches a length of nearly 4 feet (1.2 m) and a weight of 44 pounds (20 kg). Nevertheless, the dolphin catfish has an unassuming diet consisting of plant fragments and debris filtered out of mud, along with any other tiny creatures it can find. In keeping with its predominantly soft diet, the dolphin catfish—or mother of snails catfish or black doradid, as it is also known—has very weak teeth or no teeth at all. It does, however, have a long snout with a downward-pointing mouth with which it can plow into fine-grained sediments. Gut analysis has shown that among

the large quantities of mud vacuumed into the stomach there are items as varied as decomposing leaves, midge and mayfly larvae, small shrimp, and snails. Some reports also indicate that the species feeds on flower buds, fruits, and seeds.

Liberal amounts of debris are also taken into the mouth of the dolphin catfish when it sucks its food in, so it needs to separate the edible food material from the inedible matter. The dolphin catfish does this by using a unique arrangement of taste bud-covered tentacles on the roof of the mouth, supplemented by shorter ones on the floor of the mouth.

Large but Peaceful

Like all other doradids, the dolphin catfish has formidable defenses in the form of its head shield, thorny body plates, and stout, serrated dorsal and pectoral fin spines. In addition, any predator would be faced with the sheer physical size of the fish—in itself an excellent deterrent against most attackers. Yet despite its impressive size and fearsome armory, the dolphin catfish is a genuine gentle giant.

In fact, the dolphin catfish is so peaceful and tolerant of other species that even small fish can be housed safely with it in a suitably large aquarium. Indeed, it is the dolphin catfish that requires protection from more aggressive species of catfish and cichlids, even if they are only a fraction of its size. The dolphin catfish is

Thorny Split

Despite the diversity of size and shape that exists within the family Doradidae, the 80 to 100 species can be split into just two groups according to the shape of their heads. The broad-headed species, in which the head is wider than it is high, all have three pairs of simple barbels. The group includes the raphaels, such as the striped raphael, plus the snail-eating catfish (*Megalodoras irwini*). The second group, known as the narrow-headed species or the narrow-breasted species, have a head that is higher than it is wide. They also have three pairs of barbels, but they are often elaborate. The group includes the zipper, sierra, or mouse cats, such as the dolphin catfish.

The striped raphael (**Platydoras costatus*****) is a broad-headed doradid that lives in the middle Amazon River region. It has a robust, strong body protected by rows of thorny plates typical of the species.***

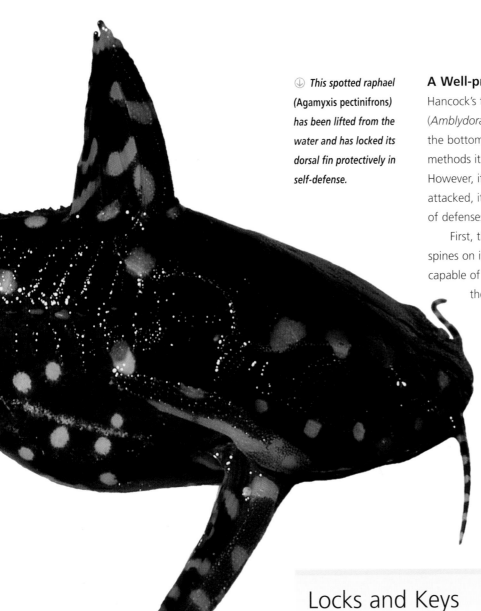

⊕ *This spotted raphael (Agamyxis pectinifrons) has been lifted from the water and has locked its dorsal fin protectively in self-defense.*

A Well-protected Talker

Hancock's talking catfish, or Hancock's doradid (*Amblydoras hancocki*), usually lies placidly on the bottom, giving no indication of the various methods it can employ to defend itself. However, if this small catfish is picked up or attacked, it unleashes a remarkable battery of defenses.

First, there are sharply pointed, saw-edged spines on its dorsal and pectoral fins, both capable of inflicting painful stab wounds when they are raised. Next, it has the ability to clamp its pectoral fins shut with such force that they, too, can cause considerable pain to an attacker. There are also spines on the gill covers and hard body plates (scutes) with sharp, backward-pointing thorns.

At the same time, the fish can produce croaking sounds that may be amplified under water, perhaps sufficiently to scare off a would-be attacker. Furthermore, glands located at

a shy creature that spends most of the daylight hours sheltering in a chosen spot that it will use on a daily basis.

It is a creature of habit that appears to prefer familiar surroundings. Owing to its large size, it is usually left undisturbed under its favorite log, ledge, or cave, where its size and formidable defenses act as effective deterrents. However, if the dolphin catfish feels threatened and decides to stand its ground rather than flee or make way, it simply shakes its body, sending out an unmistakable message that it wants to be left alone. Faced with such an imposing image, most intruders move off.

Locks and Keys

Many catfish, including doradids such as the dolphin catfish, are not only able to raise their dorsal and pectoral fin spines in defense but can also lock them in an upright position. Once they are raised, the spines cannot be lowered forcibly. Therefore, if a catfish with such fins finds itself inside the mouth of a predator, it extends the dorsal and pectoral fins, and then no amount of chewing or pressure on the part of the predator will force the fins to fold and so provide a more palatable mouthful.

For the pectoral fin spines the locking mechanism consists of specially modified bones that must be rotated backward in their sockets: clockwise for the left fin spine and counterclockwise for the right fin spine. Once the bones are rotated, the fins can be folded back into the normal position. The dorsal fin spine cannot, however, be rotated. Instead, there is a latch that holds the spine erect; and when it is raised, it releases the spine, thus allowing the fish to fold its dorsal fin.

Nemadoras humeralis *is a typical narrow-headed doradid; note the elaborate barbels divided into barblets.*

the base of the pectoral fins can produce a milky fluid. At first, the substance was believed to be secreted only under stress. However, it has also been reported in doradid catfish that are under no stress of any kind. It is therefore not clear what conditions trigger the secretion. Although the milky fluid is known not to cause an irritation on undamaged skin, it is thought that it may cause a burning sensation if it comes into contact with an open wound. However, no experiments have so far been carried out to test the theory. We do not know if it tastes foul either.

If the secretion does have the properties described above, then it could be used in conjunction with the spiny fins, thorny body scutes, and other forms of defense. For example, if a predator pounces on a doradid

Many-named Doradid

Amblydoras hancocki has numerous common names, no doubt a reflection of its wide distribution in tropical South America. In English alone it has at least ten names: talking catfish, Hancock's doradid, false talking catfish, croaking spiny catfish, purring catfish, Hancock's amblydoras, blue-eye catfish, striped doras, striped doradid, and flying pan catfish (probably a misspelling of frying pan catfish, an alternative name best reserved for the banjo catfish of the family Aspredinidae).

Although the name that has become most widely accepted is talking catfish, this is, perhaps, one of the least appropriate. A. hancocki certainly talks; in fact, it is one of the most talkative species in the whole family. However, since there are also numerous other talkers within the Doradidae, it would probably be more accurate and less ambiguous if we were to refer to this beautiful fish as either Hancock's doradid or Hancock's amblydoras.

catfish and in biting or attempting to swallow it gets its delicate mouth tissues punctured by one of the spines or other sharp defensive structures, it could receive a spurt of irritating, foul-tasting secretion. Surprised at having taken in such an unexpectedly unpalatable and painful mouthful, many predators are likely to choose the easiest and safest option and spit out their intended meal.

Driftwood catfish (*Trachelyopterus galeatus*)

Common name Driftwood catfish (woodcats)

Family Auchenipteridae

Order Siluriformes

Number of species About 65–75 in 21 genera

Size Most about 6 in (15 cm) in length or less, some barbelless species around 21.7 in (55 cm)

Key features Head may be flattened; has stout, bony plates (cephalic or nuchal shield) that extend to front edge of dorsal fin; usually 3 pairs of barbels, with maxillary ones fitting into groove under eye; barbelless species (sometimes classified as a separate family: the Ageneiusidae) have 1 pair of short barbels; body scaleless; lateral line organ has rough zig-zag or irregular pattern; dorsal and pectoral fins have prominent spine at front; adipose fin small or lacking; well formed caudal, anal, and pectoral fins

Breeding Internal fertilization typical, several hundred eggs laid

Diet Predatory; feed on smaller fish and insects

Habitat Mostly nocturnal, spending day resting in holes in wood or rocks, in slow-flowing habitats; some, like ageneiosids, found in midwater in large rivers

Distribution South America from Panama southward to Argentina

⤒ *The driftwood catfish or common woodcat (Trachelyopterus galeatus) becomes increasingly dark with age. It gets its name because its coloration makes it resemble a piece of wood. The fish is widely distributed in the Amazon region from the northern tip of South America to tropical Peru.*

CATFISH

Driftwood Catfish

Auchenipteridae

Driftwood catfish have a surprising and unusual breeding behavior. Like live-bearing fish, they mate by fertilizing their eggs inside the body.

DRIFTWOOD CATFISH ARE UNIQUE AMONG catfish families in having internal fertilization, although it is quite common among some sharks and is found in all the so-called live-bearing fish. Some fin modifications are essential for internal fertilization to happen. The modifications occur either in males, in females, or in both sexes. In driftwood catfish both males and females have evolved the necessary changes to allow sperm to transfer from inside the male's body to inside the female's body.

In mature males the genital opening is not located on the belly itself, as in all other catfish, but at the end of a tube that extends along the front edge of the anal fin. Modifications on the anal fin ray support the tube, enabling it to be flexed during actual mating, thus providing a covered "corridor" for the sperm to travel along. In females the modifications consist largely of an indented area around the genital opening that can accommodate the tip of the male's modified anal fin.

Changing with Age

As males mature, the spine at the front of the dorsal fin grows and becomes stouter than in the females. The maxillary (upper jaw) barbels also change from being short, soft, slender structures into larger, stiffer, and broader ones. The changes occur as the anal fin also becomes modified to act as the mating organ.

During the breeding season the changes become more pronounced, with the dorsal fin spine itself developing small, fine spines in some species. The barbels also become particularly stiff and may develop tubercles. The top of the head and the dorsal fin spine may also become covered in the spawning or nuptial tubercles.

⤓ *The midnight, or zamora, woodcat (Auchenipterichthys thoracatus) grows to about 4.5 in (11 cm) when mature. It feeds on small fish and insects and is typically found in the Amazon River system in South America.*

 SEE ALSO Guppies, Swordtails, and Lampeyes 38:94

Unique Breeders

After a preliminary courtship in which the male chases the female, the two fish move close to each other. The male then uses his dorsal fin spine, stiff barbels, and tubercles to secure a good hold on the female and maneuver into a position from which he can introduce the tip of his modified anal fin into the female's opening.

Actual contact lasts only a few seconds, during which sperm transfer takes place, but the actual spawning embraces can last considerably longer. In some of the driftwood catfish of the genera *Trachelyopterus* and *Parauchenipterus*, for example, they can last 10 to 20 seconds, while in the barbelless catfish they can last as long as several minutes.

Spawning embraces can even occur over a period of a day, after which the female will retain the fertilized eggs inside her body for as long as several weeks. A few hundred eggs are then released spread over the substratum or among plants. The eggs take about one further week to hatch, during which time they can swell to about twice their original size. There is no parental care during this phase.

The above description of mating behavior is a generalized account derived from the information we have about a number of driftwood catfish. Details are not, however, available on the spawning habits of all the 65 or so species making up the family.

Other Names

Driftwood catfish are also known as woodcats. They are so called because of their habit of squeezing into holes in sunken logs or rocks. Another explanation for the description woodcats is because the coloration and shape of some species resemble branches or other pieces of wood.

Red-tailed catfish (*Phractocephalus hemioliopterus*)

Common name Antenna catfish (long-whiskered catfish)

Family Pimelodidae

Order Siluriformes

Number of species Around 300 in 56 genera

Size From 3.2 in (8 cm) to 10 feet (3 m)

Key features Body form and coloration very diverse; general features: elongated scaleless body; 3 pairs of long barbels (nasal barbels absent); terminal (or almost terminal) mouth in all but 2 species; adipose fin and forked caudal fin present in all species except one; well-formed eyes except for a few cave species that are eyeless

Breeding No documented accounts currently available

Diet Fish; carrion; human waste; larger species may eat other animals such as small monkeys

Habitat Most prefer the bottom zone of flowing waters; a few inhabit caves or subterranean watercourses

Distribution Widely in central and South America extending northward to the southernmost regions of Mexico

↑ The red-tailed catfish (Phractocephalus hemioliopterus) has been a victim of commercial overexploitation, and numbers are dwindling. Although extremely predatory, this beautiful fish is a great favorite with enthusiasts and collectors. It is found in the wild in Peru, Brazil, Guyana, and Venezuela.

CATFISH

Antenna Catfish Pimelodidae

Although the flesh-eating piranha probably tops the list of unpopular fish among the fishermen of the Amazon River, three catfish species come close to matching it. One, known by river communities as pintadinho, piracatinga, or pirate catfish, is nicknamed the "vulture of the water."

THE PINTADINHO (*CALOPHYSUS MACROPTERUS*) is a medium-sized member of the antenna catfish family—so called because of their immensely long barbels. Unique among the family, however, the pintadinho has numerous narrow cutting teeth, while all its other relatives have either velvety (villiform) teeth or rasplike pads. The design of the pintadinho's teeth allows it to bite and tear off chunks of flesh almost as efficiently as the piranha.

Opportunistic Survivors

The arrangement of the pintadinho's teeth may be an adaptation for feeding on carrion rather than on live animals or fish. Even so, fishermen often find that their catches, whether caught on hook and line or in nets, have been attacked and partially or totally devoured by pintadinhos and their two catfish partners in crime, whale catfish (family Cetopsidae) and parasitic catfish (family Trichomycteridae). Even worse, pintadinhos and their associates swim around in schools and can work together to completely destroy a potentially excellent catch in a matter of minutes.

From the catfish's point of view the ability to quickly grab a valuable, protein-rich meal is a tremendous asset, especially during the dry season. When water levels are low, fish may die as a result of lack of water, scarcity of food, or an inability to gain access to normal food supplies. Being able to exploit the carrion that such conditions often create, and being able to do it in turbid water with poor visibility, means that pintadinhos may be more likely to survive at the expense of less versatile competitors.

↑ The shovelnose catfish Sorubim lima, found in the Magdalena and Plata Rivers of South America. The genus gets its name from the shape of its long, flattish head.

An Identity "Crisis"

The antenna catfish, also known as the pims or long-whiskered catfish, constitute one of the three largest catfish families. With around 300 species it is the largest of the scaleless or naked-skinned catfish families. In addition to the 300 or so species others are awaiting description, and several new types are discovered every year. The total number of pims is therefore on the increase.

Even if no further species were discovered, a family as large and as widely distributed as this is likely to contain fish of great diversity in size, overall shape, and habits. It is therefore very likely that if a major review were to be carried out, we would end up with quite a different organization of the family and with some groups perhaps being taken out of it altogether and being placed in the new

families. Several studies have, in fact, been carried out, with at least one of them recognizing three subfamilies: Pimelodinae, containing genera such as *Pimelodella*; Pseudopimelodinae, containing genera such as *Pseudopimelodus*; and Rhamdiinae, containing, among others, the *Rhamdia* and allied species. Others recognize them as belonging to separate families, with *Pimelodella* and *Rhamdia*, along with members of another 20 genera, belonging to the Heptapteridae, and *Pseudopimelodus*, plus four other genera, belonging to the family Pseudopimelodidae.

All members of the family share certain characteristics described in the fact panel opposite. But there are also many variations, making relationships between species and genera difficult to work out with absolute certainty in many instances. For example, the eyes can be large or small—or, in a few cases, absent. The dorsal and pectoral fins may or may not have a spine. If spines are present, they may be stout or weak; they may also be either serrated (saw-edged) or nearly smooth. The anal fin, while being well formed, can either be short, containing as few as 8 rays, or long, in which case it can contain as many as 30 rays.

Graceful, Confused Pims

The graceful pim (*Pimelodella gracilis*) is a good example of the "identity crisis." According to some scientists, *Pimelodella* is the correct name; according to others, it should belong to the genus *Pimelodus*. The distinction between the two genera is based, largely, on the shape of one of the skull bones known as the postoccipital process. However, since the shape of the bone is variable, precise identification is difficult. Therefore, this elegant 12-inch (30-cm) long catfish often appears under both names.

The same goes for another of its equally attractive relatives, the even smaller angelicus pim (*Pimelodella pictus* or *Pimelodus pictus*), and many of the other 80 or so other species that together with several other genera make up a substantial subgroup within the family.

As a group, the graceful pim and its closest relatives are more active during the evening and night than during the day. Some, such as the

"Dustbin" Vulture Catfish

While the pintadinho or piracatinga is a superefficient predator of trapped, hooked, or netted fish and a scavenger of carrion, its diet does not consist entirely, or even predominantly, of such protein-rich foods. It is, in fact, an omnivore, eating both plant and animal matter of all kinds. In many Amazonian river communities, from tiny settlements to large cities, much of the household waste is thrown into the river. Pintadinhos gather around such aquatic garbage dumps, feeding on food ranging from discarded vegetable matter to animal-based offal. It is for this reason that the species is sometimes known as the "vulture of the water."

Away from such dumps the pintadinho has been found to feed on fleshy fruits, particularly during the high-water season when they are abundant. Crabs and small fish, along with some carrion, have also been found among the stomach contents of the few specimens that have been studied.

⊕ *An imitator catfish (Brachyrhamdia imitator) from South America showing the characteristic, well-developed adipose fin.*

angelicus pim, are active during the daylight hours. Most species have the long, flowing barbels that give the family its common name.

Closely related to *Pimelodella* and *Pimelodus* is the genus *Rhamdia*. Like its two cousins, *Rhamdia* has a well-developed adipose fin that adds grace and beauty to the overall profile. About 60 species are currently placed within the genus. However, once a review is carried out, and some species are reallocated, the number will decrease significantly.

Long-whiskered Giants

Pride of place in terms of barbel development undoubtedly belongs to some of the shovelnosed pims. They are called shovelnoses because of their flattened heads. One species, the spotted or porthole shovelnose (*Hemisorubim platyrhynchos),* has a lower jaw that extends beyond its upper jaw, making it even more shovel-like in appearance.

Some species are not only attractively colored or patterned but boast exceptionally long maxillary (upper jaw) barbels that extend well beyond the tail. Examples include the sturgeon catfish (*Platystomatichthys sturio*), which can grow to around 26 inches (66 cm), and members of the genus *Platysilurus,* for example, the Malarmo antenna catfish (*P. malarmo*).

The shovelnoses also produce the largest pims, although other family members also grow to substantial sizes. For example, the red-tailed catfish (*Phractocephalus hemioliopterus*) can reach about 5 feet (I.5 m) in length and weigh around 180 pounds (80 kg).

The giant among giants, however, is the piraíba (*Brachyplatystoma filamentosum*), reportedly able to grow to nearly 10 feet (3 m) in length. Such large specimens are rare, but individuals over 6.5 feet (2 m) long and weighing in at 240 pounds (110 kg) are fairly common. In 1914 President Theodore Roosevelt described an Amazonian catfish that "occasionally makes prey of man." The fish was undoubtedly the piraíba. However, it is unlikely to eat humans, since its diet is mainly other fish, supplemented by small animals such as monkeys that drown after accidentally falling into the river.

Bumblebees...and Bumblebees

Some pimelodids are often referred to as bumblebee catfish. Among the best-known members in the genera *Batrachoglanis* and *Cephalosilurus* are *B. raninus* and the white-

⬆ **Pseudoplatystoma fasciatum** *from the Amazon River is another shovelnosed species, clearly indicated by its wedge-shaped head.*

Tame Six-million-year-old Cat

Although the family Pimelodidae includes members that show considerable variety in terms of their features, such as size and habits, it also contains species that have remained virtually unchanged for millions of years. Such lines, or lineages, of consistent descendency are known as "conservative." The best example of the evolutionary stability within the family is represented by the magnificent red-tailed catfish. Fossils of the species found in Venezuelan deposits dating back around 6 million years appear to be identical to the modern-day species.

Despite its large size and predatory habits, the red-tailed catfish is popular among aquarists because it retains its colorful body pattern throughout life; many catfish tend to become progressively duller with age. It is easy to keep and also very rewarding because it quickly becomes extremely tame and likes to be fed by hand, can be stroked, and can even lifted out of the water. The red-tailed catfish has become one of the few fish that can be regarded as a true companion animal—a description usually reserved for pets such as cats or dogs.

The bumblebee pim (Microglanis iheringi) is named for its stripy, beelike body pattern. Like other bumblebee catfish, it has a rounded, blunt head and tiny eyes.

edged bumblebee catfish (*C. albomarginatus*). Both have body patterns of broad, irregular, vertical dark bands on a light-colored base. The patterning is particularly well marked in small specimens. Even though the patterning may not

be the true yellow-and-black coloration of real bumblebees, it resembles the insects sufficiently to have given rise to the common name. Other pims, most notably in the genus *Microglanis*, have similar beelike body patterns. The best known of them is the bumblebee pim (*M. iheringi*), but the dwarf marbled catfish (*M. poecilus*) is also very similar.

In fact, *Pseudopimelodus* and *Migroglanis* species look so much alike, particularly during their juvenile phase, that they are often confused with each other. Fully adult specimens can be easily distinguished by their size, however: *Microglanis* attains a maximum size of only 3.2 inches (8 cm), but *Pseudopimelodus* can reach 6 inches (15 cm) in length. There are other distinguishing features, such as variations in the dentition and the lateral line, but they require close examination for the differences to be appreciated.

The Asiatic bumblebee catfish of the Bagridae family look very similar, but can easily be told apart by their nasal barbels, which bumblebee pims do not have.

Blind Pims

There appears to be a species of antenna catfish adapted to almost every ecological niche, including caves. There is, for example, a pink-bodied, eyeless pim in Guacharo Cave in Suriname. It was originally named *Caecorhamdia urichi*, but it is more likely to be an eyeless form of *Rhamdia quelen*, familiar in neighboring rivers. The supposed existence of a wide range of intermediates between the two forms in the cave indicates that this may be the case. Currently, however, opinion seems to be leaning toward regarding it as a subspecies: *R. quelen urichi*.

São Paulo, Brazil, is home to another pink-bodied, eyeless pim, *Pimelodella kronei*. In many other respects this fish is so similar to the fully eyed, fully colored *Pimelodella lateristriga* that the blind species is believed by some authorities to be a variant form, known as *P. lateristriga* var. *kronei*.

Also from the São Paulo area comes *Caecorhamdella brasiliensis*, which some authorities have variously considered to be a valid genus and species or a variant form of a fully eyed, fully colored species. Today, however, it is considered to be *Pimelodella kronei*.

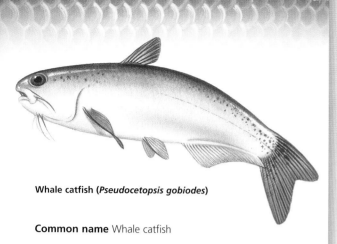

Whale catfish (*Pseudocetopsis gobiodes*)

Common name Whale catfish

Family Cetopsidae; 4 species of *Helogenes* are sometimes considered as a separate family: the Helogeneidae, or marbled catfish

Order Siluriformes

Number of species Around 12–23 in 4–7 genera according to classification system used

Size Range from about 0.7 in (1.8 cm) to about 10.4 in (26.4 cm)

Key features Usually large, rounded head with small eyes; powerful jaws armed with numerous small teeth, located slightly under tip of snout; body smooth with no scales; 3 pairs of barbels (no nasal barbels); adipose fin absent (except in some *Helogenes*, where presence or absence can vary within a single species)

Breeding Habits are unknown

Diet Exclusively carnivorous: large fish and mammals

Habitat Mostly in turbid waters and on sandy and muddy substrata

Distribution Tropical South America

⬆ *The whale catfish* Pseudocetopsis gobiodes *grows to about 6 inches (15 cm) in length. It is found in Brazil, Paraguay, and Argentina, but like many other whale catfish its biology is little known.*

Whale Catfish

Cetopsidae

Whale catfish get their common name because when the first species was discovered, it was thought to resemble a miniature whale.

AMAZONIAN FISHERMEN ARE SOMETIMES ALARMED to find that their quarry is attacked by another fish while being hauled from the water. They may be even more surprised to discover their catch fish has a hole in its belly, and that there is a live fish inside still feeding! Such instances are, in fact, remarkably common. What is more surprising is that the voracious fish that attacks with such ferocity is not a piranha but a whale catfish. Whale catfish are members of the family Cetopsidae, some members of which have the scientific name *Cetopsis*, meaning "whalelike."

Curious Predatory Cats

Whale catfish, or cetopsids, are perhaps the least catfishlike species in the order. They have very small eyes (a condition known as microphthalmic), scaleless bodies, three pairs of barbels, a highly reduced swim bladder, and no adipose fin. Although such features are unusual in a catfish, what really sets whale catfish apart are their predatory habits. Strong teeth and streamlined, smooth skin allow them to open up large holes in the bodies of their prey and slip inside. Indeed, they are so voracious that in addition to attacking fish, whale catfish that have been attracted to bait, a dead fish, or some other prey can be lifted out of the water still attached firmly to their victim. They are often so intent on gorging themselves that it is possible to lift a piece of bait or a carcass out of the water with the whale catfish going about its business as if nothing has happened.

Cetopsids are generally found along the sandy or muddy bottom of rivers, where sediment-laden water makes it impossible to see further than a few inches at a time. Under such conditions eyesight is quite unimportant, so the fact that the fish are microphthalmic

⬇ *The blue whale catfish (Cetopsis coecutiens) grows to about 10.4 inches (26.4 cm). Only a few of the whale catfish are well known; we have very few details regarding their lifestyles.*

 SEE ALSO Catfish, Antenna **37**:84; Catfish, Parasitic **37**:94; Piranhas, Silver Dollars, and Pacus **38**:42

Candirú and Cindirú

Whale catfish are frequently referred to in their native lands as candirú or carneros (*carne* is Spanish for meat). However, there are also other catfish referred to by the same common names. They belong to a totally separate family, the parasitic catfish (Trichomycteridae). The best-known of the parasitic catfish is *Vandellia cirrhosa*, a tiny fish that feeds mainly on blood extracted from the gills of its victims, but which is also known to follow a stream of urine and enter the urethra (urinary tract) of the animal or human responsible for producing the stream. The biology and lifestyle of the candirú is discussed more fully in the section describing the parasitic catfish, the family Trichomycteridae.

hugging habits, in fighting constantly against the current.

Turbid-water Specialists

In parts of the Brazilian Amazon whale catfish form shoals with three other catfish species. They are the highly predatory pintadinho or piracatinga (*Calophysus macropterus*) in the family Pimelodidae—which can grow to nearly 20 inches (50 cm) in length—plus two much smaller species of parasitic catfish from the family Trichomycteridae. Together the fish attack not only their own prey but also cause havoc among fishermens' catches. This is especially true in turbid water, where the fish appear to hold an advantage over piranha, which dominate in clear-water habitats. In fact, whale catfish are only infrequently found in clear water.

It is possible that their turbid-water adaptations become particularly valuable as water bodies shrink during the dry season, resulting in cloudy water conditions and greater availability of dead fish and other animals caused by the less favorable conditions at such times of the year. The abundant source of high-protein food is exploited to the full by cetopsids at a time when other fish are starving and choking to death.

does not place them at any disadvantage to the other river inhabitants when it comes to searching out food.

Once they find an adequate food source, the nourishment they obtain from one large, protein-rich meal will sustain them for a considerable period—particularly since cetopsids appear not to use much energy in either swimming around or, due to their bottom-

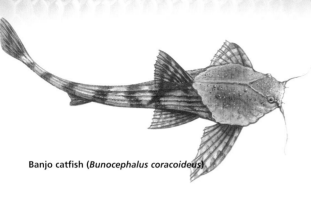

Banjo catfish (*Bunocephalus coracoideus*)

Common name Banjo catfish (frying pan catfish)

Family   Aspredinidae

Order   Siluriformes

Number of species Around 29 in 12 genera

Size   Most under 6 in (15 cm); largest can grow to 16.5 in (42 cm)

Key features Head and anterior part of body flattened and much broader than the rest of body; posterior half of body narrow and elongated; body scaleless, containing numerous tubercles; gill openings reduced to slits; adipose fin lacking; anal fin has 50–60 rays in the Aspredininae, 5–18 rays in the Bunocephalinae

Breeding Information scarce; reports refer to several thousand eggs being laid by some species of Bunocephalinae, such as the frying pan catfish (*Bunocephalus coracoideus*), in a depression excavated by male; eggs are protected by male; in Aspredininae the eggs become attached to the abdomen of the female via a thin stalk containing blood vessels; developing embryos possibly receive food by this route; similar arrangement reported in sea catfish (family Ariidae) that inhabit similar estuarine habitats

Diet   Mainly bottom-dwelling invertebrates, especially worms

Habitat   Bunocephalinae generally found in shaded waters close to water currents, on fine-grained substratum with some leaf litter; Aspredininae found closer to coasts, in muddy brackish or marine waters; Hoplomyzontinae strictly freshwater species preferring vegetated waters

Distribution Widespread in tropical South America

⬆ *The 4.7-inch (12-cm) long banjo catfish (Bunocephalus coracoideus) lies buried in silt, where its excellent camouflage helps conceal it. The species is also called the frying pan catfish.*

Banjo Catfish

Aspredinidae

Banjo catfish are so named because they are shaped like miniature banjos. But unlike a banjo, these catfish hide an amazing secret that is revealed at times of danger—jet propulsion.

THE BANJO CATFISH FAMILY IS SPLIT into three further subfamilies. The Aspredininae contains long-tailed species in which the anal fin contains between 50 and 60 rays. There are three genera in the subfamily: *Aspredo*, *Aspredinichthys*, and *Platystacus*. Within the subfamily is found the largest member of the family, the slender banjo catfish (*Aspredo aspredo*), which grows to 16.5 inches (42 cm). The subfamily Bunocephalinae consists typically of short-tailed species in which the anal fin contains between five and 18 rays. There are five genera, including *Amaralia* and *Bunocephalus*, with a total of around 20 species. The remainder belong to the subfamily Hoplomyzontinae.

A Quick Getaway

Banjo catfish have two gill openings, reduced to narrow slits. The fish spend most of the day at rest or swimming lazily among the leaf litter on the bottom, and for such activity the slits are perfectly adequate for expelling the gentle flow of water that washes over the gills. However, they are unsuited to cope with larger water volumes, such as those demanded by prolonged periods of intense activity. Not surprisingly, therefore, banjo catfish are lethargic fish that do not burn up energy looking for food or chasing rivals or potential mates.

But there are circumstances that call for a quick getaway, such as when a banjo fish is being eyed by a potential predator. When that happens, the catfish's instinct is to remain totally still, relying on its excellent camouflage. Should this trick fail and a rapid exit become necessary, the fish takes in a gulp of water and snaps its mouth shut. The action creates a sudden buildup of pressure inside the mouth

⬇ *The banjo catfish Bunocephalus amaurus. The shape of aspredinids also gives rise to their other common name: frying pan catfish.*

cavity. The catfish then forcibly ejects the water through its tiny gill slits. The thrust so created catapults the catfish forward with such speed that it is propelled, sometimes literally, out of the "jaws of death." Each jet-propelled hop takes the banjo catfish only a little distance forward. Nevertheless, several spurts in quick succession can make for a very effective escape.

Mysterious Shedders

As banjo catfish became more popular as aquarium fish, enthusiasts started becoming concerned by incidents of skin shedding, even among healthy specimens. Pieces of skin were noticed in tanks where banjos were kept with other fish; and when banjos were kept on their own, the fragments were often larger.

Several theories were put forward as possible causes. Low acidity or a buildup of bacteria in the water were two of the reasons suggested. Gradually, though, it became

evident that banjos were shedding their skin on a more or less regular basis.

We now know that both banjos and members of the Asian family Akysidae—known as stream catfish or Asian banjos, owing to their overall similarity—shed their skin both in the wild and in aquariums. The occurrence of smaller bits of skin in aquariums that banjos shared with other fish turned out to be the result of the banjos' tank mates eating the shed skin, causing it to fragment. The occurrence of larger fragments in tanks where banjos were kept alone was due to the fish ignoring their shed skin, leaving it intact.

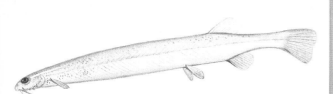

Candirú (*Vandellia cirrhosa*)

Common name Parasitic catfish (pencil catfish, spiny-headed catfish)

Family Trichomycteridae (Pygidiidae)

Order Siluriformes

Number of species Around 155 in 36 genera

Size From 0.8 in (2 cm) to around 6 in (15 cm)

Key features Elongate, some species eel-like—particularly parasitic types; some free-living species resemble loaches (family Cobitidae); number of barbels vary: at least 2 pairs; most species possess pelvic fins, but absent in at least 6 genera; gill covers carry spines

Breeding No details available

Diet Small invertebrates; parasitic types feed on blood or on scales and body mucus of other fish

Habitat Predominantly bottom dwellers; parasitic types and a few others, such as *Tridentopsis*, frequent midwater levels more regularly; some prefer clear, cool, flowing waters

Distribution Widely distributed in South America

⬆ *The parasitic candirú (Vandellia cirrhosa) is only 1 inch (2.5 cm) long. It lives in rivers and streams in the Amazon basin.*

Parasitic Catfish

Trichomycteridae

Some parasitic catfish species behave like underwater vampires. They may look quite elegant, but they can present a serious and painful threat to their unfortunate victims.

NOT EVERY SPECIES IN THE FAMILY Trichomycteridae is parasitic; in fact, only the representatives of two of the eight subfamilies exhibit parasitism. In total they account for just under 50 of the 155 or so species of trichomycterids. However, they are the most famous, and the name parasitic catfish has therefore virtually superseded the other name for the family, the pencil catfish, although the latter is perhaps more representative of the group as a whole.

➔ **Trichomycterus maculatus** *is a free-living, nonparasitic species.*

Special Adaptations

Generally, members of the family are elongate catfish with at least two pairs of barbels; the nasal barbels are usually present, while the chin (mental) barbels are usually absent. At least six genera have lost their pelvic fins, while most have lost their adipose fin. The gill covers are usually adorned with spines; they are

Trichomycterid Subfamilies

Subfamily	Approx. No. Genera (Species)	Type of Lifestyle
Copionodontinae	2 (3)	nonparasitic
Trichogeninae	1 (1)	nonparasitic
Trichomycterinae	6 (88)	nonparasitic
Stegophilinae		
Pareidontinae	10 (30)	parasitic
Vandelliinae	5 (18)	parasitic
Tridentinae	4 (6)	nonparasitic
Glanapteryginae	4 (5)	nonparasitic
Sarcoglanidinae	4 (4)	nonparasitic

Some estimates place the total number of species at over 175

particularly useful as "hooking-on" structures in some of the genuinely parasitic species. One of the best-known species of South American parasitic catfish is the candirú or carnero (*Vandellia cirrhosa*). In true vampire fashion the candirú feeds on blood. It usually finds its food by sensing the minute current of water produced by the gill plates of a potential victim (another fish) as they flap open and shut during breathing. The candirú swims toward the current and, at the precise moment when the gill plate is open, dives into the gill chamber. There it attaches itself to the gills, rasps away the delicate tissue, and drinks the blood that oozes from the wound.

Any strongish, narrow current will elicit the homing-in response, not just respiratory currents, as many unfortunate visitors to candirú waters have found to their cost when they have decided to empty their bladder in an infested river. Sensing the warm current of urine as the bladder is emptied, the candirús swim up the current and into the first available orifice, and then painfully sink their gill cover spines into the surrounding tissue. Once lodged inside the urinary tract, they rasp away the internal surface tissue and begin their blood-sucking activities.

Apparently, it is possible to prepare a potion from certain tropical fruits that will cause the attached pencil-like catfish to release its grip. Unfortunately, even after taking the potion, it will be several hours before the catfish can be passed.

After learning this painful lesson through bitter experience, the men of tribes bordering candirú-infested waters wear special protective penile sheaths. However, there do not appear to be equivalent protective devices for women.

A Painful Experience

Although it was widely reported that the candirú can enter the urinary tract of humans, some people found it difficult to accept. The river people and jungle dwellers who sometimes encounter this tiny catfish knew it only too well, however, although the fish presented more of a threat to cattle during river crossings.

Then, in the early 1990s the following headline appeared in *A Critica*, a newspaper published in Manaus at the mouth of the Rio Negro, Brazil: "Doctor Removes Candirú from a Patient in Manaus." It told of a young boy who was swimming in a river in Itacoatiaru, some 108 miles (175 km) from Manaus. He had removed his swimming trunks to urinate and was attacked by a candirú. Apparently, this did not cause any pain at first, only discomfort. The pain came later.

Eventually, the catfish died and began to decompose, thus increasing the risk of serious consequences. The urologist who handled the case had learned something about candirú and proceeded to extract the parasitic catfish, via an endoscopy, in an operation lasting two hours. During the operation he cut off the fish's spines and then delicately extracted the body (and the spines) using fine forceps. A few days later the patient was well enough to leave the hospital, having learned a painful and embarrassing lesson.

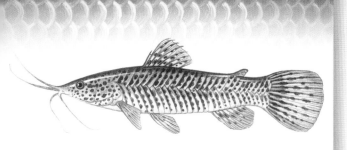

Slender armored catfish (*Callichthys callichthys*)

Common name Armored catfish (callichthyid armored
catfish)

Family Callichthyidae

Order Siluriformes

Number of species 208 in 8 genera

Size From around 1.25 in (3 cm) to 8.8 in (22 cm)

Key features All callichthyids have 2 rows of overlapping
bony plates on body; up to 2 pairs of well-
developed barbels and fleshy flaps or other
extensions on lower lip; in Callichthyinae snout
more or less depressed (flattened from top to
bottom); mouth on underside of snout; in
addition to barbels around the mouth a pair of
threadlike outgrowths on upper jaw and fleshy
flaps on lower lip; in Corydoradinae snout
rounded or compressed (flattened from side to
side); small mouth under tip of snout; no
threadlike processes present on upper jaw

Breeding Callichthyinae build bubble nests for eggs that
are guarded by male; Corydoradinae fertilize
eggs uniquely, eggs abandoned after laying;
eggs hatch in 3–4 days in both subfamilies

Diet Wide range of invertebrates and plant debris

Habitat Fast-flowing to still waters; most are bottom-
hugging species, but there are a few exceptions

Distribution Tropical regions of South America

⊕ *The slender armored catfish (Callichthys callichthys) is
immediately recognizable by its unusual, plated scales. This
species often forms shoals and is common in South America.*

Armored Catfish

Callichthyidae

*The first armored catfish imported in 1880
immediately caught the public imagination. Since that
time their endearing behavior and appearance have
made them firm favorites among aquarists.*

THE ARMORED CATFISH ARE DIVIDED into two
subfamilies. The Corydoradinae, or plated
catfish, contains three genera and close to 200
species. The Callichthyinae, also confusingly
called armored catfish, contains five genera and
at least eight species.

A Good Impression

The first armored catfish imported from South
America was the peppered catfish (*Corydoras
paleatus*), a member of the plated catfish
subfamily. It has attractive body mottling, and
the males have a very long dorsal fin; but they
are not its main attractions. A pointed snout
with long, twitching barbels, big, friendly looking
and highly mobile eyes—that frequently "wink"
at you—added to the way they scuttle around
on the bottom in groups fascinated the first
collectors to set eyes on the fish.

The characteristics are often referred to as
"endearing" and "comical," terms that reveal
some of the main reasons that lie behind our
admiration for the catfish. It is an admiration
that makes them probably the best-known fish
in the order Siluriformes. In fact, the fish do
not, of course, do anything for "endearing" or
"comical" reasons; it just happens that their
natural behavior appeals to humans.

Over the years many other *Corydoras*
species have been imported for the aquarium
hobby, and the ongoing interest in the genus
on the part of enthusiasts the world over has
led to the scientific community having a ready
supply of new species to study. As a result, the
body of scientific data that we possess on
Corydoras and its relatives is massive.

 SEE ALSO Catfish, Suckermouth Armored **37:**104

Armor-plated Catfish Families

Members of the family Callichthyidae can be distinguished from all other catfish by having two rows of overlapping bony plates that run along each side of the body. The "armor plating" has given rise to the most frequently used common name for the family—the armored catfish.

However, strictly speaking, there are four catfish families whose members also carry "armor" in the form of bony plates. Since all possess other identifying characteristics, we can give each its own common name. Thus the Callichthyidae are called callichthyid armored catfish; the Loricariidae are known as suckermouth armored catfish; the Doradidae are called thorny catfish; and the Scoloplacidae are called spiny dwarf catfish.

Adaptable Survivors

Both subfamilies of callichthyid catfish share a number of features in addition to the two rows of bony plates. For example, the swim bladder is encased in bone. Many species can also use their intestine as a respiratory organ that allows them to take in air at the water surface and pass it down the gut, where the oxygen can be extracted. This makes it possible for these hardy catfish to survive in conditions that would kill many other aquatic creatures. Such a remarkable ability, allied to strong spines on the pectoral fins (there are also prominent spines at the front of the dorsal and adipose fins), permits many callichthyids to migrate over land from ponds that are drying up or are polluted in search of better conditions.

Provided the air is humid and the soil

⊕ *The peppered catfish (Corydoras paleatus) is a member of the subfamily of armored catfish known as the plated catfish. It has become one of the most popular of all aquarium species.*

conditions not dry, callichthyids can travel considerable distances, protected not just by their ability to take air directly into their gut but also by their armor, which helps reduce loss of water from the body surface. It also acts as a very effective deterrent against predators, especially when the fin spines are erected.

Even in unfavorable conditions armored catfish are excellent survivors because they eat almost anything.

⊕ *The largest of the corydoras is the banded corydoras (Corydoras barbatus) from southeastern Brazil. It reaches about 5 inches (13 cm) in length.*

A Mystery Solved

Armored catfish have two basic breeding strategies. In the Corydoradinae the sticky eggs are laid on a rock, plant, or log surface and then abandoned. Members of the subfamily Callichthyinae, for instance, *Dianema* and their relatives, build bubble nests—constructed by the male—into which the eggs are deposited and guarded by the male.

During courtship corydoras females can be observed aligning themselves at right angles to the males in what is known as the T-position. Once appropriately aligned, a female will nudge the anal region of her mate. Next, she releases a small batch of eggs into a pouch created by her pelvic fins. Then she rests on the bottom for about a minute before swimming to a chosen spawning site where she will attach the eggs and abandon them.

However, what baffled many scientists and aquarists was exactly how the eggs were fertilized. Did the males simply release sperm

The Cory "Wink"

Catfish do not have eyelids and cannot wink. Yet this is precisely one of the features of corydoras (or corys, as they are affectionately known) that makes them so popular with fish fanciers. When we examine the "winking" behavior in detail, we quickly discover that what we humans interpret as a wink is not a wink at all.

What corydoras do is rotate their eyeballs, perhaps in order to clean them, since they live on the bottom where detritus, mud, and general debris can coat the eye surface. The action, which can be completed in a matter of a second or two, consists of moving the eyeball downward in its socket. As that is done, the pupil and iris of the eye (the parts visible when the eye is in its normal position), disappear momentarily from view as the rotation takes them below the lower rim of the eye socket. As they disappear, the surrounding tissue—which is shiny and reflective—becomes visible. This is the "eyelid" that appears to close and then reopen when the eyeball is rotated back into position, creating the illusion of a wink.

Therefore, when a cory looks at its keeper through the glass front of an aquarium and winks, it is not, as some people would like to believe, relating to or bonding with its keeper, it is merely cleaning its eyes.

into the water and fertilize the eggs? Or did the sperm reach the belly of the female during the T-position? Or was there some other method that brought sperm and egg together?

In the end the answer came through some simple observations carried out on the bronze corydoras (*Corydoras aeneus*) in 1995 at Osaka University, Japan. The path followed by sperm was determined by releasing a jet of methylene blue (a harmless dye) in front of a courting female's snout as she nudged the vent of the male. After about four seconds the female produced a jet of similarly colored water from her vent. The blue water was then funneled into the pelvic fin pouch and was followed, a few seconds later, by the release of eggs.

This remarkable observation, allied to the fact that females were seen to keep their gill covers shut while "drinking"' in the T-position, led researchers to conclude that bronze corydoras females fertilize their eggs by first drinking the sperm released by their mates. Since the T-position is known to be part of the breeding ritual of over 20 species of corydoras, it is assumed that this method of insemination is not unique to the bronze corydoras.

Corydoradinae Species

Corys and their immediate relatives are small, social fish that live in groups, often consisting of more than one species. When not swimming in open water, they scuttle along the bottom. Their popularity has never waned since the first specimens were introduced, initially to Europe and then to the U.S., between 1880 and the early years of the 20th century.

Today, there are cory fanciers all around the world. Over 135 species and subspecies of the fish have been described, and more than 45 additional ones are awaiting description. About 30 of the described species have only rarely been seen, but of the remainder well over 100 have been kept in aquariums at one time or other. The peppered corydoras and the bronze corydoras are still the most popular. They are bred in large numbers by commercial fish farmers, and they are available either in their

wild-colored form or as albinos (with a pinkish-white body with pink eyes). Despite the fascination that exists for corys, most of the other species in the subfamily are primarily kept by specialist enthusiasts and in relatively small numbers.

Although *Corydoras* is by far the largest genus in its subfamily, there are two further, closely related genera: *Aspidoras* with about 18 species and *Brochis* with three species. *Aspidoras* species are generally smaller and more slender than *Corydoras*, although the distinction is not immediately obvious in some species. In *Aspidoras* the eyes are small, and the dorsal and pectoral fin spines are short and thick when compared with those of *Corydoras*. However, the most distinctive features, the cranial fontanels, cannot be seen in living specimens. (A fontanel is a skin-covered space found between some of the skull bones.) In *Aspidoras* there are two small fontanels, while in *Corydoras* and the other genus in the subfamily, *Brochis*, there is only one, much larger fontanel.

Brochis species look rather like bronze corydoras, but they are stockier and larger, with some specimens growing to around 4.7–5 inches (12–13 cm); bronze corydoras rarely

⊕ *Adolfo's corydoras (Corydoras adolfoi) comes from the Upper Rio Negro River, Brazil. It is about 2.8 inches (7 cm) in length.*

exceed 2.8 inches (7 cm). *Brochis* species also have more rays in the dorsal fin: between 10 and 18 rays, compared with 6 to 8 rays in *Corydoras* species.

Rainy Season Spawners

Spawning in most plated catfish species occurs with the start of the rainy season. This varies with geographical location, but the two periods of greatest activity are August to October and December to March. Aquarists and commercial breeders often artificially create the natural conditions of the rainy season. Sometimes they carry out a partial change of the aquarium or pond water, which results in lowering the water temperature by a few degrees— mirroring what happens in the rainy season. Alternatively, or in addition, they spray water onto the surface of the water, helping fool the fish into believing that the spawning season has arrived.

Once the biological reproductive rhythms have begun, there is no stopping corys intent on breeding, and they seem oblivious to everything else going on around them. Ripe females are incessantly pursued by hyperactive males that may only interrupt their chases in order to display in front of their prospective mates.

Eventually, the chasing stops and

⊕ *The porthole catfish (Dianema longibarbis) is an elegant, long-whiskered species with a plainish tail. Its closest relative, the flagtail catfish (D. urostriata), has a bolder marked tail.*

fertilization and egg laying begins. Part of the reproductive cycle includes adopting the characteristic T-position already described. During this phase the female drinks her mate's sperm and releases it, a few seconds later, into the pouch or "basket" created by her pelvic fins into which she has previously released a few eggs. The female may be held in the T-position for up to a minute by the male clasping her barbels with his strong, often saw-edged pectoral fin spine.

Once the female is released, she will deposit her adhesive eggs among vegetation or on some other solid surface. The total number of eggs can vary from between 30 to 800 depending on the species and size of the individual female. Hatching can take up to eight days—again depending on the species as well as on water temperature.

Callichthyinae Species

Compared with their "plated" cousins, the members of the subfamily Callichthyinae—often referred to as hoplos—are large fish. The cascudo hoplo (*Hoplosternum littorale*), for instance, can grow to 8.8 inches (22 cm), making it the largest of the callichthyid armored catfish.

Up to 1997 there were only four genera in the armored catfish subfamily. One of them, *Hoplosternum*, contained three species, but there had long been debate over their inclusion within the genus because of wide variations in their geographical distribution as well as differences in body shape and size. Eventually, scientists concluded that the three species should be split up into three separate genera. It has even been suggested that the splitting should go a stage further, resulting in several species within not just the genus *Hoplosternum* but also within the genus *Callichthys*.

In the subfamily two species, the porthole catfish (*Dianema longibarbis*) and the flagtail or stripetail catfish (*D. urostriata*), are generally more slender and more active during the day than the hoplos (*Hoplosternum*, *Lethoplosternum*, and *Megalechis* species) or the slender armored catfish or cascarudo (*Callichthys callichthys*). Even so, their period of greatest activity begins at dusk and continues into the night. The two species have lighter "armor" than their relatives and particularly long, whiskerlike barbels that they tend to hold out horizontally. The flagtail catfish also has—in keeping with its name—a strikingly marked caudal fin.

The cascarudo and hoplos, for their part, are stockier fish that spend much of the daytime resting on the bottom, usually under logs or in crevices. They are heavily armored fish that show extreme variation in coloration and size, and it is these factors, allied to the shape

A pair of albino bronze corydoras (Corydoras aeneus) adopting the T-position during spawning, in which the female (on right) aligns herself at right angles to the male.

Armored Catfish

Although there is no universal agreement regarding the number of species in the subfamily Callichthyinae, the following list is the one that is becoming most widely accepted.

Common Name	Scientific Name	Approx. Size Inches (cm)
Armored catfish or cascarudo	*Callichthys callichthys*	8 (20) max.
	C. fabricioi	4.9 (12.5)
Porthole catfish	*Dianema longibarbis*	4 (10)
Flagtail or stripetail catfish	*D. urostriata*	4.75 (12) max.
Cascudo hoplo or hassar	*Hoplosternum littorale*	8.75 (22) max.
Striped hoplo	*H. magdalenae*	3.8 (9.6)
	H. punctatum	3 (7.7)
	Lethoplosternum altamazonicum	2 (5)
	L. beni	2 (5)
Dwarf or spotted hoplo	*L. pectorale*	6 (15) max.
	L. tordilho	1.8 (4.6)
	Megalechis personata	4.9 (12.4)
Port or spotted hoplo	*M. thoracata*	7 (18)

A further species that is mentioned in both scientific and aquarium literature, *Cataphractops melampterus*, is now believed to be the same species as the cascudo hoplo or hassar.

*The dwarf or spotted hoplo (*Lethoplosternum pectorale*) can be distinguished by its rounded caudal fin.*

of the tail, that have led to the division of opinion regarding the number of species.

However, whether the tail is distinctly rounded (as in *Callichthys*), gently rounded (as in *Lethoplosternum*), more or less straight (as in *Megalechis*), or even slightly forked (as in *Hoplosternum*), none has the beautifully forked tail found in both the porthole catfish and the flagtail catfish.

Grunting Bubble Nesters

Exceptionally for catfish, hoplos and their relatives build bubble nests at the water surface. The nests are made from mucus-covered bubbles, produced through the gill covers after air is gulped at the surface. It is usually the male that undertakes the task, but females have also occasionally been seen to assist. Whether they do or not, there is often a great deal of contact between male and female during the building process. Males can also produce sounds at nesting time.

The nest is built among floating vegetation; but if it is not available, the male may tear pieces from submerged plants and incorporate them among the bubbles. Nests exceeding 12 inches (30 cm) in diameter and just over 3 inches (8 cm) in depth have been reported for

at least one species, the cascudo hoplo; in the cascarudo nests measuring 6 inches (15 cm) across and nearly 2.5 inches (6 cm) deep are common.

Once nest construction is complete, courtship becomes even more intense. The female will eventually release batches of 15 to 20 eggs into a pouch created by her pelvic fins and will then be rolled over on her back by the male so that her belly (and therefore the eggs) are facing his own belly, thus ensuring fertilization of the eggs. After fertilization the female swims upside down and releases the eggs among the bubbles. Up to 500 eggs have been reported depending on species, with the most prolific layers being the cascarudo and the cascudo hoplo. As egg laying goes on, and immediately afterward, males will add further bubbles to the nest.

The eggs are relatively large, measuring up to 0.08 inches (0.2 cm) across. During their incubation, which lasts three to five days depending on temperature and species, the male will defend the eggs vigorously. Males often produce grunting noises during this period, just as they did during nest construction. On hatching, the young fish will have absorbed their rich supply of yolk and will either spend a day around the nest or become independent as soon as they leave the egg.

Spotted pleco (*Hypostomus punctatus*)

Common name Suckermouth armored catfish

Family   Loricariidae

Order   Siluriformes

Number of species Around 550–600 in around 80 genera

Size   From under 2 in (5 cm) to 20–24 in (50–60 cm)
                or more in some plecos

Key features Fairly flattened or sloping head, often adorned
                with bristles in males; underslung, suckerlike
                mouth with pads containing numerous tiny
                scraping teeth; eyes possess a light-regulating
                flap; 3 pairs of barbels; body covered in
                overlapping bony plates (scutes); "chin" and
                lower surface of body flat; caudal fin usually well
                formed; dorsal, pectoral, and pelvic fins usually
                carry a stout spine

Breeding   Eggs laid in open, under shelter, or in burrows
                according to species

Diet   Most species feed on encrusting algae and
                detritus, together with attendant creatures such
                as small crustaceans and aquatic insects; also
                feed on carrion

Habitat   From lowland still waters to highland fast-
                flowing streams

Distribution Widely in Central and tropical South America

⬆ *The spotted pleco (*Hypostomus punctatus*) is found in the
lower reaches of rivers in and around Guyana. It grows to
12 inches (30 cm).*

Suckermouth Armored Catfish

Loricariidae

*Disguise is important in this large and diverse family.
Some suckermouth catfish resemble twigs, and others
are almost invisible because the sandy skin pattern
over their backs acts as a perfect camouflage.*

THE SUCKERMOUTH ARMORED CATFISH FORM the largest
catfish family. Some catfish may be described as
looking like sharks, frying pans, banjos, or
leaves, but among the loricariids there are yet
other variations. For example, those of the
genus *Farlowella* look more like twigs than fish.
Others, such as some *Rineloricaria* species, have
such perfect camouflage they become
practically invisible in their natural habitats.

All suckermouth armored catfish have the
distinctive suckerlike mouth armed with pads of
numerous, tiny teeth on the underside of the
snout. They also have bony plates on the body,
a flattened "chin" and lower part of the body,
and rough edges on some of the fins—
particularly the pectorals and pelvics. Although
such features identify them as loricariids, they
nevertheless fall into a number of distinct
subfamilies, each with its own set of features.

➔ *The suckerlike
mouth, from which the
family Loricariidae gets
its common name, is
clearly shown here.
The family has about
250–300 more species
than its nearest rival, the
antenna catfish (family
Pimelodidae).*

Wide-ranging Diversity

Size varies enormously within the family.
The smallest species occur among the
Hypoptopomatinae, where the redfin otocinclus
(*Parotocinclus maculicauda*) is fully mature at
around 1.8 inches (4.5 cm). The largest species
occur among the plecos, with some individuals
reaching 24 inches (60 cm) or more in length.

Many species are found in lowland slow or
still waters, sometimes in stagnant conditions.
Others are found in forest streams with thick,
overhanging vegetation. Yet more are found
along sandy or muddy banks of larger rivers and
also in restricted habitats with rocky and sandy

bottoms containing numerous shelters. Some also live in fast-flowing streams at altitudes up to 10,000 feet (3,000 m) that lack vegetation but contain gravel and boulders.

Feeding occurs mainly at night. During daylight most species rest on the bottom or in crevices; some are more active at dusk, while *Otocinclus* and allied species are active during the day. All are bottom dwellers with relatively poorly developed swimming ability but strong "sticking" ability due to their sucker mouths. It allows them to cling to rocks and other surfaces even in powerful currents.

Breeding habits are also diverse. Some types, like the plecos, dig burrows, while others, like the bristlenoses, may actually spawn in the open. During the breeding season the males of some loricariid species develop sexual characteristics such as bristles. However, in the bristlenoses the bristles are present throughout the year.

Suckermouth Subfamilies

Subfamily	Approx. No. Genera (Species)	Other Details
Ancistrinae	18–24 (over 175)	Includes the "bristlenoses" distinguished by males' "whiskers" around mouth
Hypostominae	18 (175)	Plecs or plecos—medium-sized to large with bony scutes on sides and back
Neoplecostominae	1 (6)	Species resemble plecos
Hypoptopomatinae	8 (56)	Includes the small, slender otos, some of which are active during daylight,
Loricariinae	35 (185)	Includes twig and whiptail catfish
Lithogeneinae	1	Subfamily appears to have links with both Neoplecostominae and hillstream catfish (family Astroblepidae)

Bristlenoses and Relatives

It is undoubtedly the "whiskered" nature of adult males that is largely responsible for endowing bristlenoses with their characterful look. Females only have modest versions of the males' adornments at best, and juvenile males only begin to grow bristles when they attain a length of around 1.5 inches (3.8 cm).

Strictly speaking, only the 50 or more species in the genus *Ancistrus* should be regarded as bristlenoses. However, since the subfamily to which they belong, the Ancistrinae, is named after the genus, some of the other 18 to 24 genera are also sometimes referred to as bristlenoses, even though the majority of them do not have bristles.

Bristlenoses can grow to around 6 inches (15 cm). Most species live exclusively in fresh water, but some can tolerate a certain amount of salt. Spawning occurs in the rainy season, with the male establishing a territory around a hollow structure such as a log. Courtship lasts from several hours to several days. Up to 200 eggs may be laid and are guarded by the male.

The snowking pleco (Liposarcus anisitsi) grows to 24 inches (60 cm) in length. At the other end of the scale some Otocinclus and Parotcinclus species are less than 2 inches (5 cm) long. The overall shape of a loricariid is such that the fish will be pushed down onto the substrate as water flows over its head and body.

Perhaps the best-known of the species are the black spiny catfish (*Acanthicus hystrix*) and the white-spot spiny catfish (*A. adonis*). However, the best-armed species are the spiny plecos like *Pseudacanthicus hystrix*, *P. spinosus,* and their closest relatives.

The genus *Peckoltia* contains some of the most striking members of the subfamily—the striped peckoltia (*P. pulcher*) being one of the most distinctive black-and-white members of the genus. Black and white coloration is also shown to beautiful effect by the zebra peckoltia, which, to confuse matters, is not a peckoltia at all but a species of *Hypancistrus* (*H. zebra*).

Chaetostoma species, of which there are about 40, are worth mentioning because of their snouts. They are small catfish measuring 4.5–6 inches (14–15 cm) in length and have a head that is almost as wide as it is long, giving some species a distinct "swollen nose" appearance. A name like the bulldog catfish (*Chaetostoma thomsoni*) says it all.

Plecos and Relatives

The vast majority of the 175 or so members of the pleco subfamily (Hypostominae) belong to the genus *Hypostomus*. While at first sight some plecos could be confused with their cousins in the bristlenose subfamily, plecos and their closest relatives cannot erect their interopercular area. Most genera contain one to three species, with a few including up to six. *Hypostomus*, however, probably has around

Hatching takes five to ten days. The male may not eat during this period and may protect the new born fry for another week or a little longer.

Panaques are often referred to as "plecos," but they are not true plecos and do not belong to the pleco subfamily, the Hypostominae. Instead, panaques belong to the same family as the bristlenoses, the Ancistrinae.

There are only about six species in the genus *Panaque*. All have typically sloping snouts and attractive eyes—bright blue in the blue-eyed pleco (*Panaque suttoni*). The eye flap typical of all suckermouth armored catfish is particularly noticeable in panaques. Panaques are also notable for their wood-chewing habits. All suckermouths have a liking for wood, but panaques seem to need it more than most.

Among the remaining genera that make up the subfamily Ancistrinae is a group of very spiny genera and species. Many of the spines, known as odontodes, occur on the snout and pectoral fins, and are of such strength and sharpness that they provide even further defenses to an already formidable armory.

Inside-out Brushes

Bristlenoses have a rather unusual weapon among their defenses. They can erect a "brush" of short, stout, hooked spines of varying lengths located between the gill cover (operculum) and the bone in front (the preoperculum)—sometimes referred to as the interopercular area. Usually, the spines are contained in a fold or sac of soft tissue, with the tips enclosed inside and therefore not visible. However, when a bristlenose is threatened or angry, it will raise the gill cover, turning the sac inside out and exposing the spines.

Mucus-feeding Plecos

In some cichlid species, most notably discus (*Symphysodon* species), pike cichlids (*Crenicichla* species), the silver angel (*Pterophyllum scalare*), and the uarus (*Uaru* species), adults produce heavy mucous body secretions during the breeding season. Newly hatched young feed on the nutritious "body milk" until they are able to fend for themselves fully and find their own food.

During the 1990s, while judging breeding-size plecos in a professional competition in Florida, it was observed that many of the newly hatched plecos that had been introduced with the parents appeared to be grazing on the body mucus produced by the adults. Closer examination confirmed that it was the case. It seems, therefore, that at least some species of pleco have evolved a similar fry-feeding strategy to that of the above-mentioned cichlids. Whether this potential exists in all species of pleco, or whether such a strategy is actually employed in the wild (the Florida observations were in an aquarium) is not known. At least three other catfish also feed their young on "body milk," but secreted from their belly region.

120, making it one of the most significant genera in the whole loricariid family.

The top of the head in *Hypostomus* species bears tough, bony plates while, in sharp contrast, the lower surface is naked, bearing neither scutes nor conventional scales. The same arrangement applies all the way down the body to the tail, although some small granular plates may be present along the abdomen.

Some plecos are large enough to be considered as food fish by some communities. Reportedly, cooked pleco is very tasty. The smallest plecos are only around 5.5 inches (14 cm) long, but the largest, which includes the best-known species of all, the plecostomus of the aquarium hobby (*H. plecostomus*), can attain some 24 inches (60 cm) or more. Other large plecos are the members of the genera *Glyptoperichthys* and *Liposarcus*.

→ *The chubby bristlenose (*Ancistrus *species) is found in Brazil. Bristlenoses are named for the bristly, filamentous outgrowths on the snouts of males.*

In plecos, spawning occurs in deep burrows excavated in muddy river banks by the male; some of the burrows can be up to 5 feet (1.5 m) long. Up to 500 eggs are laid right at the end of the burrow, and they are protected by the male until they hatch. Shortly afterward the young adopt a feeding strategy unknown in other catfish (see box "Mucus-feeding Plecos.")

Algae-eating Otos

The otos and their allies (subfamily Hypoptopomatinae) are small fish; none exceed 6 inches (15 cm) in length, and many, like the dwarf otocinclus (*Otocinclus affinis*), are even smaller. Otos spend most of the daylight hours attached by their sucker mouths to broad leaves, often on the upper surface, and seem to tolerate daylight better than other loricariids. Nevertheless, otos are more active during the evening and night. They are particularly efficient algae eaters and are much appreciated by aquarists as biological algae controllers.

Twigs and Whips

The twig and whiptail catfish (subfamily Loricariinae) include some species that have such efficient camouflage that they become practically invisible as they lie totally motionless against the substrate. The twig or stick catfish of the genus *Farlowella* are perhaps the best

mimics of all, appearing to all intents and purposes as twigs rather than fish, especially when resting on branches. The whiptails of the genus *Sturisoma* also mimic twigs, but their mimicry is often based more on coloration than body shape. Among whiptails belonging to the genus *Rineloricaria* there are some species whose coloration matches that of coarse sand or gravel so well that it is possible for a predator to miss a fully adult specimen even when only a few inches away.

In many members of the subfamily the males develop distinctive bristles on both sides of the snout and the top surface of the pectoral fin spine and rays. Some may also have bristles along the top of the head and just in front of the dorsal fin. During the breeding season the differences can become more pronounced.

Usually, the sticky eggs are laid on a hard surface, often under cover in caves or crevices, and are guarded by the male. In some species a male will attract a series of females to his selected spawning site and will end up guarding several batches of eggs at differing stages of development.

⊖ *The sticklike* **Farlowella knerii** *hides from its enemies by disguising itself among twigs and other aquatic objects.*

⊖ *Red sailfin pleco (Pterygoplichthys gibbiceps) from Peru. Plecos can be distinguished from bristlenoses by their more pointed snouts and larger tooth pads.*

Lippy Breeders

While most members of the subfamily Loricariinae produce adhesive eggs that are laid on a hard surface and guarded by the male, some species take paternal care a significant step further.

In such species, belonging to the genera *Loricariichthys* and *Pseudohemiodon*—and possibly others—the eggs become attached in a single, elongated, flattish mass two or more eggs in thickness to the underside of the back edge of the male's lower lip. Several hundred eggs from a single female can be carried in this way, with the front portion of the egg clutch attached to the lip and the rest trailing backward along, but not attached to, the belly. Early reports indicating that the eggs might also be attached to the belly of some *Loricaria* males have not been confirmed.

The attachment of the eggs is quite loose, as a result of which some may become dislodged through sudden movements or accidental rubbing against submerged objects. It is not known if any dislodged eggs are subsequently picked up again by the male.

Glossary

Words in SMALL CAPITALS refer to other entries in the glossary.

Abbreviated heterocercal term used to describe a HETEROCERCAL TAIL in which the upper lobe is less extended than in a typical heterocercal tail

Adaptation features of an organism that adjust it to its environment; NATURAL SELECTION favors the survival of individuals whose adaptations fit them to their surroundings better than other individuals

Adipose fin fatty fin located behind rayed DORSAL FIN in some fish

Adult fully grown animal that has reached breeding age

Agonistic any activity, aggressive or submissive, related to fighting

Air bladder see SWIM BLADDER

Ammocete larva filter-feeding lamprey LARVA

Ampullae of Lorenzini jelly-filled tubes on the head of sharks and relatives; responsible for detecting weak electrical impulses

Anadromous term describing a SPECIES that spends part of its life in the sea and part in freshwater habitats

Anal fin FIN located near the anus

Appendicula outgrowths from the umbilical cord of some sharks; appendicula enhance an embryo's ability to absorb UTERINE MILK

Aquatic associated with, or living in, water

Arborescent organ treelike modifications of GILL tissues found in air-breathing species like walking catfish

Atriopore small aperture in lancelets corresponding to the atrial, or exhalant, SIPHON in sea squirts

Barbel whiskerlike, filamentous sensory growth on the jaws of some fish, including catfish

Benthic occurring, or living, on the bottom

Brackish water water that contains salt in sufficient quantities to distinguish it from fresh water but not enough to make it sea water; brackish water is found in estuaries, mangrove swamps, and other habitats where fresh water and sea water mix

Branchiostegal rays flattish, riblike bones located ventrally behind the GILL covers and making up the floor of the gill chamber

Brood offspring of a single birth or clutch of eggs

Brood pouch structure formed from FINS or plates of a parent fish in which fertilized eggs are placed to hatch safely

Bubble nest nest of bubbles that harbors eggs or offspring of some fish

Camouflage markings or features of a creature that aid concealment

Carnivore creature whose diet consists exclusively of other animals

Cartilaginous formed of cartilage

Catadromous term describing a SPECIES that migrates from fresh water to the sea for spawning

Caudal fin "tail" FIN

Caudal peduncle part of the body where the tail begins

Caudodorsal term describing an extension of the CAUDAL FIN onto the back of the body; this fin contains RAYS but no spines; caudodorsal fins are found in catfish of the family Plotosidae

Cephalic shield head shield formed by bony plates, as found in upside-down catfish

Cephalofoil term used to describe the "'hammer" of hammerhead sharks; thought to provide lift and maneuverability

Cerebellum part of the hindbrain involved in the coordinated activity of muscles, posture, and movement

Cerebral hemispheres pair of symmetrical, rounded, convoluted tissue masses that form the largest part of the brain in many organisms, e.g., mammals

Chordata PHYLUM of animals having a single, hollow dorsal nerve cord, a NOTOCHORD, GILL SLITS, and a postanal tail; some of these characteristics may only be present in the earliest stages of development

Chromatophore pigment-containing cell whose shape or color can be altered

Chromosome tiny, rod-shaped structure in the cell NUCLEUS; chromosomes contain DNA, which carries genetic information

Cilium (*pl.* **cilia**) tiny, hairlike structure growing out from the surface of some cells; cilia are capable of whiplike actions and can facilitate movement

Cirrus (*pl.* **cirri**) hairlike or tentaclelike growth, e.g., as found on the nostrils, supraorbital area, and nose in some blennies

CITES Convention on International Trade in Endangered Species; an agreement between nations that restricts international trade to permitted levels through licensing and administrative controls; rare animals and plants are assigned categories

Claspers structures between the PELVIC FINS of male cartilaginous fish that allow them to clasp a female during mating, and that facilitate the transfer of sperm

Class taxonomic level below PHYLUM and above ORDER

Cloaca single chamber into which anal, urinary, and genital ducts (canals) open

Clone identical cell or individual derived from a single cell, e.g., an egg

Community all the animals and plants that live together in a HABITAT

Compressed term used to describe a structure that is flattened from side to side

Cone cone-shaped light-sensitive cell in the retina of the eye; cones are particularly sensitive to colors (see ROD)

Copepoda subclass of small crustaceans, some of which are parasitic; copepods do not have a hard carapace (shell) but have a single, centrally placed eye

Cosmoid scale type of SCALE found in many fossil and some primitive fish

Countershading color distribution seen in many fish in which the back is darker than the belly

Crepuscular active at twilight

Cryptic coloration camouflage-type coloration that helps organisms blend in with their surroundings; some species are cryptically colored at all times, while others, e.g., many squirrelfish, are cryptic during the day and more brightly colored at night

Ctenoid scale similar to the CYCLOID SCALE but with a toothed posterior edge rather than a smooth or wavy (crenulated) one

Cusp point or prominence, often on a tooth

Cycloid scale thin, flexible overlapping scale, roughly the shape of a human finger nail, found in modern bony fish and the primitive bowfin (*Amia calva*); the front edge of each scale is embedded in a special pouch in the surface of the skin; the back edge is free and smooth or wavy (crenulated) but not toothed as in CTENOID SCALES

Dendritic finely branched

Denticle small, toothlike scale found in sharks and some of their closest relatives (see PLACOID SCALE)

Depressed term used to describe a structure that is flattened from top to bottom

Detritus debris consisting of fragments of dead plants and animals

Dimorphism existence of two distinct forms

Dioecious having separate sexes (see HERMAPHRODITE)

Display any fairly conspicuous pattern of behavior that conveys specific information to others, usually to members of the same species; often associated with "courtship" but also in other activities, e.g., threat displays

Diurnal active during the day

DNA (deoxyribonucleic acid) the substance that makes up the main part of the chromosomes of all living things; DNA is the carrier of genetic information

Dorsal relating to the upper surface

Dorsal fin(s) FIN(S) on the back of a fish

Electrocyte electricity-generating cell, usually consisting of a modified muscle cell

Electroplaque stack or column of ELECTROCYTES; also referred to as electroplates

Endangered species SPECIES whose POPULATION has fallen to such a low level that it is at risk of EXTINCTION

Endemic term used to describe a SPECIES that is found in just one country or area

Endostyle longitudinal mucus-secreting groove found in the pharynx of sea squirts and relatives, lancelets, and lamprey LARVAE

Endothermic term used to describe animals that can generate internal body heat, e.g., mammals, birds, and certain fish like large tunas or some species of sharks

Erectile capable of being raised

Esca modified fleshy tissue on the tip of the first RAY of the DORSAL FIN (ILICIUM) in marine anglerfish; the esca resembles a small piece of "bait" that, when waved in the water, attracts PREY toward the anglerfish

Estivation dormancy or torpor during summer periods of heat and drought

Evolution development of living things by gradual changes in their characteristics as a result of MUTATION

Exotic term used to describe a SPECIES that is found in locations outside its natural distribution range, usually as a result of intentional or accidental introduction

Extant term used to describe SPECIES that are still in existence

Extinct term used to describe SPECIES that are no longer in existence

Extinction complete dying out of a SPECIES

Falcate sickle-shaped, as in the PECTORAL FINS of thresher sharks

Family group of closely related SPECIES (e.g., piranhas) or a pair of fish and their offspring

Fin winglike or paddlelike organ attached to certain parts of the body of a fish or other aquatic animals and used for steering, locomotion, and balance

Fontanel space or gap between some bones of the skull

Food chain sequence in which one organism becomes food for another, which in turn is eaten by another

Fry young fish

Fusiform body shape that tapers at both ends, i.e., spindle shaped

Ganoid scale SCALE found in most extinct ray-finned fish (Actinopterygii) consisting of a thick enamel-like layer underlaid by a dentine layer and a basal bony layer

Genus (*pl.* **genera**) group of closely related SPECIES

Gill organ by which a fish absorbs dissolved oxygen from the water and gets rid of carbon dioxide

Gill raker bristlelike extensions on the gill arches of filter-feeding fish; used for trapping suspended food particles in the water as it passes from the mouth via the GILLS and, subsequently, to the exterior through the GILL SLITS

Gill slit slit between the GILLS that allows water through

Gonopodium modified ANAL FIN of male LIVEBEARERS used to inseminate females

Habitat place where an animal or plant lives

Harem breeding "unit" consisting of a single male and several females, as in boxfish

Hemoglobin pigment that gives blood its red color; hemoglobin is used to carry oxygen around the body

Herbivore animal whose diet consists exclusively of plants

Hermaphrodite organism having both male and female reproductive organs

Heterocercal term used to describe a tail (CAUDAL FIN) in which the upper lobe contains the tip of the vertebral column (backbone); in such fins the upper lobe is usually considerably larger than the lower lobe

Holotype specimen on which the scientific description of a SPECIES is based; also referred to as the TYPE SPECIMEN

Hybrid offspring of a mating between two different SPECIES

Hydrostatic organ organ used in controlling flotation or buoyancy

Hypertrophy excessive growth as a result of an increase in cell size

Hypocercal term used to describe a tail (CAUDAL FIN) in which the lower lobe contains the end tip of the NOTOCHORD; in such fins the ventral (lower) lobe is usually larger than the dorsal (upper) one

Ichthyologist scientist specializing in the study of fish

Ilicium first modified ray of the DORSAL FIN in marine anglerfish, usually located on top of the head and bearing a fleshy tip (ESCA) used to lure unsuspecting victims toward the waiting anglerfish

Inferior mouth mouth located below the snout

Interoperculum bone joined anteriorly to the preoperculum and posteriorly to the interoperculum ligament, which, in turn, is connected to the OPERCULUM (gill cover)

Introduced describes a species that has been brought from places where it occurs naturally to places where it has not previously occurred

Invertebrate general term used to describe an animal that lacks a backbone

IUCN International Union for the Conservation of Nature, responsible for assigning animals and plants to internationally agreed categories of rarity (see table beow)

Juvenile young animal that has not reached breeding age

Krill tiny, shrimplike crustacean

Labyrinth organ respiratory organ found in gouramis and their relatives; formed from modified GILLS and housed in a chamber in the top of the gill cavity

Larva first stage of some fish SPECIES; newly hatched INVERTEBRATE

Lateral relating to the sides

Lateral line organ series of small fluid-filled pits linked to tubes that, in turn, are linked to a common canal; the lateral line detects movements (vibrations) in the water

Leptocephalus elongate, highly compressed, ribbonlike LARVAL stage of some fish such as eels

Livebearer SPECIES in which males introduce sperm into the body of the female, resulting in internal fertilization; developing embryos are generally retained by the female until birth

Macula neglecta part of the inner ear of sharks and related fish; important in sound perception

Melanoblast cell in which melanin (dark pigment) is formed

Mermaid's purse term used to describe the hard, leathery egg cases of sharks, skates, and rays

Metamorphosis changes undergone by an animal as it develops from the embryonic to the ADULT stage

Microphthalmic having tiny eyes

Migration movement of animals from one part of the world to another at different times of year to reach food or find a place to breed

Milt fluid containing male sperm

Monotype sole member of a GENUS

Monotypic GENUS or FAMILY that contains a single SPECIES

Mouthbrooder SPECIES in which the eggs are incubated in the mouth of one or other of the parents, according to species; FRY may also be protected this way

Mutation change in the genetic material (DNA) that, in turn, results in a change in a particular characteristic of an individual cell or organism

Nape the back of the neck

Naris (*pl.* **nares**) alternative word for nostril(s)

Nasopharyngeal duct nasal opening (nostril) in hagfish; also called the nasohypophysial opening

Natural selection process whereby individuals with the most appropriate ADAPTATIONS survive to produce offspring

Nematocyst stinging cell of sea anemones, jellyfish, and their relatives

Neoteny retention of larval characteristics into the sexually mature adult stage

Neural spine bone extension on the upper (dorsal) surface of individual vertebrae (back bones)

Niche part of a HABITAT occupied by a SPECIES, defined in terms of all aspects of its lifestyle (e.g., food, competitors, PREDATORS, and other resource requirements)

Nocturnal active at night

Notochord "rod" of cells along the back during the early stages of embryonic development in chordates; the notochord is replaced by the spinal column in all but the most primitive chordates

Nucleus dark, dense structure found in living cells of higher animals and plants, but not in bacteria; the nucleus contains the CHROMOSOMES, which, in turn, contain genetic information in the form of DNA

Nuptial tubercle small, whitish, pimplelike growth developed by males during the breeding season, usually on the snout, head, cheeks and PECTORAL FINS; nuptial tubercles are known in at least 25 families of fish

Olfactory relating to the sense of smell

Olfactory bulb outgrowth from part of the lower anterior margin of the brain; responsible for detecting smells; also known as the OLFACTORY LOBE

Olfactory lobe see OLFACTORY BULB

Olfactory sac highly folded "chamber" in front of the OLFACTORY BULB; sensitive to smells

Omnivore animal whose diet includes both animals and plants

Operculum bone forming the gill cover in fish

Orbital relating to the eyes

Order level of taxonomic ranking

Organ of Hunter organ consisting of ELECTROCYTES that generate powerful electric pulses

Organ of Sachs organ consisting of ELECTROCYTES that are capable of generating weak electric pulses

Osmoregulation control of water balance in the body

Osmosis passage of molecules from a less concentrated to a more concentrated solution through a semipermeable membrane

Otolith grain of calcium carbonate in the semicircular canals of the ear; vital for balance

Oviparity egg laying; eggs and sperm are usually released into the environment where external fertilization takes place; in sharks the term is retained, although fertilization is internal

Ovipositor breeding tube extended by a female to place her eggs in a precise location

Palate roof of the mouth

Papilla (*pl.* **papillae**) small, usually cone-shaped projection

Parallel evolution development of similarities in separate but related evolutionary lineages through the operation of similar selective factors

Parasite organism that derives its food, for part or the whole of its life, from another living organism (belonging to a different SPECIES); parasites usually harm the organism on which they feed (the host)

Parasphenoid long, ridgelike bone with two side "arms"; located on the underside of the skull, this bone forms the "crucifix" in the crucifix fish (*Arius* spp.)

Pectoral fin one of the paired FINS connected to the pectoral girdle

Pelvic fin one of the paired FINS connected to the pelvic girdle

Pharyngeal slit alternative term for GILL SLIT

Pharyngeal teeth teeth located in the throat area and used primarily for grinding or crushing food

Pheromone substance released in tiny quantities by an animal and detected by another of the same SPECIES

Photophore luminous organ possessed by many deepwater bony and cartilaginous fish

Phylum (*pl.* **phyla**) group of animals whose basic or general plan is

IUCN CATEGORIES

EX **Extinct**, when there is no reasonable doubt that the last individual of a species has died.

EW **Extinct in the Wild**, when a species is known only to survive in captivity or as a naturalized population well outside the past range.

CR **Critically Endangered**, when a species is facing an extremely high risk of extinction in the wild in the immediate future.

EN **Endangered**, when a species faces a very high risk of extinction in the wild in the near future.

VU **Vulnerable**, when a species faces a high risk of extinction in the wild in the medium-term future.

LR **Lower Risk**, when a species has been evaluated and does not satisfy the criteria for CR, EN, or VU.

DD **Data Deficient**, when there is not enough information about a species to assess the risk of extinction.

NE **Not Evaluated**, species that have not been assessed by the IUCN criteria.

similar, and which share an evolutionary relationship, e.g., the Chordata

Phytoplankton see PLANKTON

Piscivore animal whose diet consists exclusively of fish

Placenta spongy, blood-rich tissue found in mammals and some fish, such as livebearing sharks, by which oxygen and nutrients are supplied to—and waste products are removed from—embryos during development

Placoid scale small toothlike SCALE, often referred to as a DENTICLE, found in sharks; it consists of a bonelike basal part embedded in the skin and a backward-directed free, pointed border or spine covered in an enamel-like substance; placoid scales do not increase in size as the shark grows: instead, they are replaced throughout life

Plankton term used to describe the generally minute animals (zooplankton) and plants (phytoplankton) that drift in marine and fresh water

Plica fold or wrinkle, e.g., on the skin or a membrane

Poikilothermic term used to describe animals whose body temperature matches that of the environment, e.g., most fish, amphibians, and reptiles; such animals are frequently—but inaccurately—referred to as cold-blooded

Polyp individual animal making up a colony, as in corals; polyps have a tubular body, usually topped by a tentacle-ringed mouth, giving the animal the appearance of a miniature sea anemone

Polyploidy process by which cells possess three or more full sets of chromosomes

Population distinct group of animals of the same SPECIES or all the animals of that species

Postanal tail tail whose base originates behind the anus

Predator animal that hunts and kills other animals for food

Preoperculum anterior bone of the gill cover

Prey animal hunted for food

Proboscis elongated trunklike snout or projection

Protandrous hermaphrodite hermaphrodite that goes through a male phase before becoming a female

Protogynous hermaphrodite hermaphrodite that goes through a female phase before becoming a male

Protractile describes any structure that can be lengthened by, e.g., being pushed out, as spiny-finned fish are able to do with their mouths

Race see SUBSPECIES

Radial muscle muscle associated with the FIN RAYS of the head (known as radials)

Range geographical area over which an organism is distributed

Ray small spine that acts as a support for the FIN membrane

Recruitment addition of new individuals to a population, usually by reproduction or by inward migration from another population

Refractive index degree by which light rays are "bent" as they pass from one medium to another, e.g., from air to water

Rete mirabile dense network of blood vessels found in certain animals; heat exchange can occur between blood across this network allowing, e.g,. some sharks to retain body heat and maintain their internal temperature at a higher level than that of the surrounding water

Retina inner, light-sensitive layer of the eye on which images are formed

Reverse countershading type of color distribution seen in fish SPECIES that habitually swim upside down, e.g., some members of the Mochokidae; in these fish the belly is darker than the back, i.e., it shows the opposite color distribution found in normally COUNTERSHADED fish

Rod rod-shaped light-sensitive cell in the retina of the eye; rods are particularly sensitive to discerning shapes, especially in dim light (see CONE)

Rostral associated with a snout or ROSTRUM

Rostrum snout

Rugosity term used to describe rough or wrinkled tissue

Scale one of the usually tough, flattish plates that form part of the external covering of most fish species

Scatophagous term used to describe an animal that feeds on waste materials like sewage or feces; best-known fish exhibiting this trait are the scats

Scute platelike, modified scales found in some fish, including catfish

Semicircular canal fluid-filled canal in the inner ear; semicircular canals are set at right angles to each other, contain OTOLITHS, and are essential in maintaining body balance

Shell gland gland possessed by female sharks, skates, and rays; responsible for secreting the outer egg casing known as a MERMAID'S PURSE

Siphon funnel-shaped structure through which water can be taken in (inhalant) or discharged (exhalant)

Spawn eggs of a fish; the act of producing eggs

Species a POPULATION or series of populations that interbreed freely but not normally with those of other species

Specific gravity (**SG**) "weight," or density, of a liquid compared with pure water at 39.2° F (4° C); pure water has an SG value of 1.000, while the SG of seawater is around 1.020

Spiracle porelike opening associated with the GILLS

Spiral valve spiral infolding of the intestinal wall in primitive fish like sharks and rays

Standard length (**SL**) length of a fish measured from the tip of the snout to the CAUDAL PEDUNCLE

Stridulation vibration or rubbing together of two surfaces to produce a sound; in fish it usually refers to rubbing together of bones or fin spines, e.g., in some filefish and triggerfish

Stripping removal of eggs and sperm from ripe fish by the application of gentle pressure along the abdomen

Suborbital located under the orbit, or eye socket

Subphylum grouping of organisms sharing a number of characteristics in addition to those shared by members of a PHYLUM; examples of a subphylum are the sea squirts and relatives (Urochordata) and the backboned animals (VERTEBRATA), which together form the phylum CHORDATA

Subspecies subdivision of a SPECIES that is distinguishable from the rest of that species; often called a RACE

Substrate bottom of an aquatic HABITAT

Subterminal located underneath the end or tip, e.g., a subterminal mouth is one located underneath the tip of the snout

Suprabranchial chamber cavity or space above the gill chamber; the suprabranchial chamber houses the suprabranchial organ, i.e., modified gill tissues used by air-breathing fish, such as walking catfish

Supraorbital located above the orbit, or eye socket

Suture line along which two or more bones are immovably joined, as in the skull

Swim bladder gas-filled sac found in the body cavity of most bony fish; the amount of gas in the swim bladder can be regulated, allowing the fish to rise or sink in the water

Symbiosis relationship between two unrelated organisms from which both parties benefit, e.g., the light-producing bacteria that flashlight fish have in special cheek pouches (light organs); organisms that live in this manner are referred to as symbionts

Symphysis junction between the left and right sides of the jaw, i.e., where both bones meet and fuse at the front

Tapetum lucidum layer of light-reflecting tissue located under the retina; it amplifies the amount of light entering the eye and assists vision under poor light conditions

Taxonomy studying, naming, and grouping of living organisms; also termed classification

Tendril entwining, fiberlike extension on some shark and ray egg cases that allows the eggs to attach themselves to underwater objects like seaweeds

Terminal located at the end or tip, e.g., a terminal mouth is one located at the tip of the snout

Territory area that an animal or animals consider their own and defend against others

Thermocline zone between warm surface water and colder deeper layers

Tholichthys term used to describe the young of certain fish, notably the scats, for a period after hatching; these larvae have large heads in relation to the body and protective bony plates and spines

Thoracic describes the area in or around the chest (thorax)

Thunniform swimming swimming technique in which the tail beats rapidly from side to side, but the body remains rigid; this type of swimming is found in tunas

Tonic immobility trancelike state or hypnosis exhibited by many animals, including some sharks and their relatives

Total length (**TL**) length of a fish measured from the tip of the snout to the tip of the CAUDAL FIN

T-position position adopted by at least some *Corydoras* species during mating, in which the female aligns herself at right angles to her mate's body, with her mouth close to his genital aperture

Truncated term often used to describe a CAUDAL FIN that has a straight, or more-or-less straight, edge

Tubercle small rounded swelling, nodule, or protuberance, as found, e.g., on the body of banjo catfish

Type specimen see HOLOTYPE

Uterine milk nutritious secretions produced in the womb (uterus) of female sharks during pregnancy; developing embryos feed on these secretions

Uterus womb

Variety occasional variation in a species not sufficiently persistent or geographically separate to form a SUBSPECIES

Ventral relating to the underside

Vertebra any of the bones of the spinal column

Vertebrata SUBPHYLUM of the PHYLUM Chordata characterized, especially, by a brain enclosed in a skull (cranium) and having a backbone (vertebral column) enclosing the spinal cord

Viviparity alternative term for LIVEBEARING

Weberian apparatus series of four small bones connecting the swim bladder to the ear in some fish (superorder Ostariophysi), including the catfish

World Conservation Union see IUCN

Yolk sac source of nourishment for some FRY prior to and immediately after hatching

Zooplankton see PLANKTON

Further Reading

General

Allen, G. R., *Freshwater Fishes of Australia*, T. F. H. Publications, Inc., Neptune City, NJ, 1989

Bond, C. E., *Biology of Fishes*, Saunders College Publishing, Philadelphia, PA, 1979

Campbell, A., and Dawes, J. (eds.), *The New Encyclopedia of Aquatic Life* Facts on File, New York, NY, 2004

Gilbert, C. R., and Williams, J. D., *National Audubon Society Field Guide to Fishes*, Alfred A. Knopf, New York, NY, 2002

Hayward, P., Nelson-Smith, T., and Sheilds, C., *Collins Pocket Guide to Sea Shore of Britain and Europe,* HarperCollins, London, U.K., 1996

Helfman, G. S., Collette, B. B., and Facey, D. E., *The Diversity of Fishes*, Blackwell Scientific Publications, Cambridge, MA, 1997

Meinkoth, N. A., *National Audubon Society Field Guide to North American Seashore Creatures*, Alfred A. Knopf, New York, NY, 1998

Moyle, P. B., and Cech, J. J. Jr., *Fishes: An Introduction to Ichthyology* (4th edn.), Prentice-Hall, Inc., Upper Saddle River, NJ, 2000

Nelson, J. S., *Fishes of the World* (3rd edn.), John Wiley and Sons, Inc., New York, NY, 1994

Page, L. M., and Burr, B. M., *A Field Guide to Freshwater Fishes (North America, North of Mexico)* (Peterson Field Guide Series), Houghton Mifflin Co., Boston, MA, 1991

Paxton, J. R., and Eschmeyer, W. N., *Encyclopedia of Fishes* (2nd edn.), Academic Press, San Diego, CA, 1998

Spotte, S., *Captive Seawater Fishes*, John Wiley & Sons, Inc., New York, NY, 1992

Specific to this volume

Burgess, W. E., *Colored Atlas of Miniature Catfish*, T. F. H. Publications, Inc., Neptune City, NJ, 1992

Burgess, W. E., *An Atlas of Freshwater and Marine Catfishes: A Preliminary Survey of the Siluriformes*, T. F. H. Publications, Inc., Neptune City, NJ, 1989

Dawes, J., "Judging 'Bonuses,'" *Aqualog News, No.2*, December, 1996

Dawes, J., *Complete Encyclopedia of the Freshwater Aquarium*, Firefly Books Ltd., Richmond Hill, Canada, 2001

Ferraris, C. Jr., *Catfish in the Aquarium*, Tetra Press, Morris Plains, NJ, 1991

Glaser, U., *Loricariidae: The Most Beautiful L-numbers*, Verlag A. C. S. GmbH, Mörfelden Walldorf, Germany, 1998

Glaser, U., and Glaser, W., *Loricariidae: All L-numbers and All LDA-numbers*, Verlag A. C. S. GmbH, Mörfelden Walldorf, Germany, 1995

Glaser, U., Schäfer, F., and Glaser, W., *All Corydoras*, Verlag A. C. S. GmbH, Mörfelden Walldorf, Germany, 1996

Goulding, M., *The Fishes and the Forest: Explorations in Amazonian Natural History*, University of California Press, Berkeley, CA, 1980

Goulding, M., Leal Carvalho, M., and Feireira, E. G., *Rio Negro: Rich Life in Poor Water*, SPB Academic Publishing bv, The Hague, The Netherlands, 1988

Jinkings, K., *Bristlenoses: Catfishes with Character*, Kingdom Books, Havant, U.K., 2000

Kobayagawa, M., and Burgess, W. E. (eds.), *The World of Catfishes*, T. F. H. Publications, Inc., Neptune City, NJ, 1991

Leggett, R., and Merrick, J. R., *Australian Native Fishes for Aquariums*, J. R. Merrick Publications, Artarmon, Australia, 1987

Lever, C., *Naturalized Fishes of the World*, Academic Press, San Diego, CA/London, U.K., 1996

Merrick, J. R., and Schmida, G. E., *Australian Freshwater Fishes: Biology and Management*, J. R. Merrick Publications, North Ryde, Australia, 1984

Reebs, S., *Fish Behavior in the Aquarium and in the Wild*, Cornell University Press, Ithaca, NY, 2001

Sands, D., *Back to Nature Guide to Catfishes*, Fohrman Aquaristik AB, Jonsered, Sweden, 1997

Sands, D., *Catfishes of the World: Vols 1–5*, Dunure Enterprises, Dunure, U.K., 1983–5

Tekriwal, K. L., and Rao, A. A., *Ornamental Aquarium Fish of India*, Kingdom Books, Havant, U.K., 1999

Useful Websites

http://www.fishbase.org/home.htm
An amazing website full of information even on obscure fish

http://www.si.edu/resource/faq/nmnh/fish.htm
A useful list of alternative reference for all kinds of fish

http://www.ucmp.berkeley.edu/vertebrates/basalfish/chondrintro.html
Covers both fossil and living species, with good links

Picture Credits

Abbreviations A Ardea, London; BCL Bruce Coleman Limited; FLPA Frank Lane Picture Agency; NHPA Natural History Photographic Agency; NPL Naturepl.com; P Photomax; P.com/OSF Photolibrary.com/Oxford Scientific Films; SPL Science Photo Library
t = top; b = bottom; c = center; l = left; r = right

Jacket tl Gerard Lacz/FLPA; tr David Fleetham/P.com/OSF; bl Jeff Rotman/NPL; br Paul Kay/P.com/OSF

8–9 Max Gibbs/P.com/OSF; 10–11, 12-13 Max Gibbs/P; 12–13 Max Gibbs/P.com/OSF; 14–15 Phil Degginger/AA/P.com/OSF; 16–17 Francois Merlet/FLPA 17t Garold W. Sneegas; 18 Pat Morris/A; 19 Stan Osolinski/P.com/OSF; 20 Philip Gould/Corbis; 23,24t, 24–25, 26–27, 31 Max Gibbs/P; 33b Pat Morris/A; 33t Ben Miles, Angling Times; 34–35, 36–37, 38–39, 40–41 Max Gibbs/P; 41b D. Allison; 43c, 43b, 44-45 Max Gibbs/P; 53, 54–55 D.Allison; 54 Philip Perry/FLPA; 56–57 Max Gibbs/P; 59 D. Allison; 60–61 Max Gibbs/P; 61 Mark Deeble & Victoria Stone/P.com/OSF; 62–63 Max Gibbs/P; 65 Linda Lewis/FLPA; 66–67, 68 ANT Photo Library/NHPA; 68–69 Jim Watt/BCL; 70–71 Hans Reinhard/BCL; 72–73 Gerard Lacz/NHPA; 74–75, 76–77, 78b Max Gibbs/P; 78–79, 80–81, 82–83 D. Allison; 85, 86 Max Gibbs/P; 87 Pat Morris/A; 88–89, 91 Max Gibbs/P; 93, 95 D. Allison; 97 Max Gibbs/P; 98 Max Gibbs/P.com/OSF; 99, 100–101 Max Gibbs/P; 102 India Lewis/FLPA; 103 Max Gibbs/P; 105 Gerard Lacz/FLPA; 106–107, 108–109, 110 Max Gibbs/P

Artists
Denys Ovenden, Mick Loates, Colin Newman

Set Index

A **bold** number shows the volume and is followed by the relevant page numbers (eg., **37:** 8, 70).

Common names in **bold** mean that the fish (e.g., **shark, great white**) or group or family of fish (e.g., **sheatfish**) has an illustrated main entry in the set. Underlined page numbers (e.g., **37:** 36–37) refer to the main entry for that fish or group.

Italic page numbers (e.g., **37:** 49) point to illustrations of fish in parts of the set other than the main entry.

Page numbers in parentheses—e.g., **34:** (87)—locate information in At-a-glance boxes.

Fish or families or groups of fish with main entries in the set are indexed under their common names, alternative common names, and scientific names.

123

125

AUG 2000

Stains noted 10/16/14

Dedicated to Max the Cat.

A book for children by Milton and Shirley Glaser.

Enchanted Lion Books, New York

Apples had Teeth

IF apples had teeth, they would bite back.

IF snakes were salted, they would be pretzels.

IF watermelons had feathers, they would be cushions.

IF turtles were chickens, they would run like the dickens.

IF pickles were tickled, they would never be sour.

IF polka dots were white and buttered, they would be popcorn.

IF horses had hat racks, they would be reindeer.

IF mushrooms were hairy, they would be very scary.

IF fishes had wishes, they would stay out of dishes.

IF eggs were made of glass, you could count your chickens before they hatched.

IF a kangaroo was fond of you, he would carry your books home from school.

IF carrots were parrots, vegetable soup would be noisy.

IF a zebra wore striped pajamas, you would never know.

IF pigs wore wigs, they still wouldn't fool anyone.

IF an alligator had a handle, he would be a suitcase.

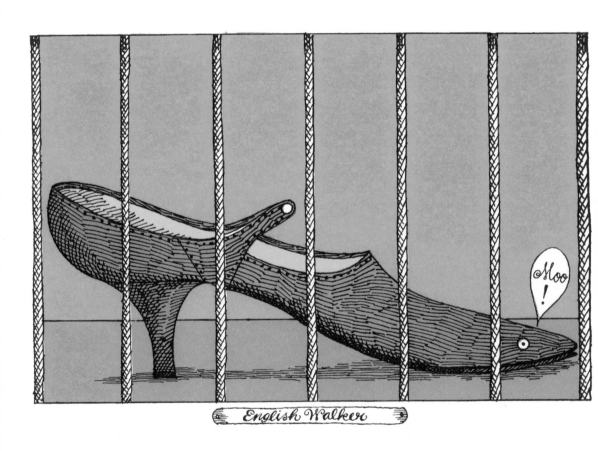

IF a shoe could moo, it would be in a zoo.

IF a grizzly bear was caught unaware, he would polish his nails and comb his hair.

IF a crab didn't grab, he would have more friends.

IF trees were pink, they would be nevergreens.

IF elephants were willing, they would be good vacuum cleaners.

IF a porcupine had a handle, he would be a scrubbing brush.

IF a bunny had money, he would buy a racoon coat.

VIA AIR SNAIL

To A Friend

IF a snail delivered the mail, he would never go out in snow or hail.

IF a rhinoceros wore a sweater, he would look a lot better.

IF you turn this page, you will see the end.

The End.

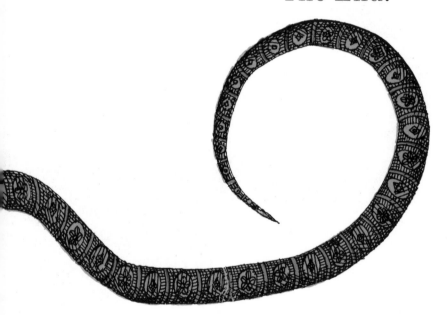

www.enchantedlionbooks.com

First Reprint Edition published in 2017 by Enchanted Lion Books,
67 West Street, 317A, Brooklyn, New York 11222
Copyright © 1960 by Milton Glaser
Copyright © for English-language edition 2017 by Enchanted Lion Books
Published by arrangement with Phileas Fogg Agency, for rights from Bruaá Editions
Color restoration: Bruaá Editions
Originally published in 1960 by Knopf, New York
All rights reserved under International and Pan-American Copyright Conventions.
A CIP record is on file with the Library of Congress
ISBN: 978-1-59270-226-8
1 3 5 7 9 8 6 4 2

IF IF IF IF IF IF

IF IF IF IF IF IF

IF IF IF IF IF IF

IF IF IF IF IF IF

IF IF IF IF IF IF

IF IF IF IF IF IF